DECLUTTER YOUR MIND

HOW TO STOP WORRYING, RELIEVE ANXIETY, AND ELIMINATE NEGATIVE THINKING

Barrie Davenport

liveboldandbloom.com

Steve "S.J." Scott

DevelopGoodHabits.com

CONTENTS

YOUR FREE GIFT

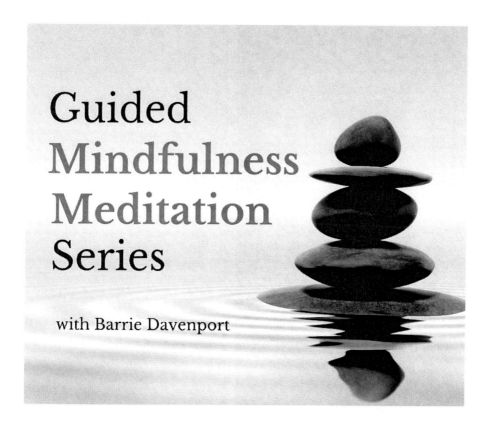

Guided
Mindfulness
Meditation
Series

with Barrie Davenport

liveboldandbloom.com/mindfulness-meditation-series

INTRODUCTION

How Thoughts Determine Our Outcomes

"Very little is needed to make a happy life; it's all within yourself, in your way of thinking."

– Marcus Aurelius

Ever feel overwhelmed by your thoughts? Do you struggle with stress or anxiety about the tasks you need to complete on a weekly basis? Do you want to simply **stop worrying about life** in general?

We all experience negative thinking from time to time. But if you often feel overwhelmed by these thoughts, then you should closely examine *what you're thinking* and how your thoughts impact your mental well-being.

This inner monologue is a natural part of your mental landscape. It's there all the time, night and day, reminding you about the groceries you need to pick up, shaming you about missing your sister's birthday, or making you feel anxious about current headlines (like politics, the environment, or the current state of the economy).

These thoughts are the background noise of your life, even though you may not always be aware of their constant presence. Take a second right now and pay attention to your thoughts. Try to stop them. It's hard, right? You'll see how they keep streaming in, one after another, unbidden and often unwanted.

Some of your thoughts are random and useless. *"My arm itches." "It looks like it's gonna rain." "Where did I put my keys?"*

On the other hand, many of our thoughts are intrusive and negative. *"That guy is a jerk." "I really screwed up that project." "I feel so guilty about what I said to Mom."*

Whether they are negative, neutral, or positive, **these thoughts clutter our minds**, just like your home can get cluttered when you have too many possessions.

Unfortunately, clearing your mental clutter isn't as simple as eliminating a possession. You can't "throw away" a thought and expect it to *stay* gone. In fact, like a never-ending game of Whack-a-Mole, your negative thoughts have a way of popping back up as soon as you slap them down.

Why We Think Negative Thoughts

Now, imagine your mind as a fully organized home—a home that's free from extraneous, draining, and useless items that agitate you. What if you could surround yourself only with thoughts that uplift, inspire, and soothe you?

Consider for a moment your mind as a peaceful cloudless sky, and you have the power to choose what floats across. If that cloudless mental sky is so desirable, then why do we think so much, with so few filters to sort the positive and necessary thoughts from the random and unnecessary?

Your brain contains about 100 billion neurons, with another billion in your spinal cord. The total number of connections between neurons— the cells responsible for processing—has been estimated at 100 trillion synapses.

Our powerful brains are constantly processing all sorts of experiences and analyzing them in the form of thoughts. Thoughts form what we perceive to be reality.

We can control and direct our thoughts, but it often feels like our thoughts have minds of their own, controlling us and how we feel. Thinking is necessary for solving problems, analyzing, making decisions, and planning, but in between the times of proactive mental endeavors, the mind roams like a wild monkey, dragging you through the brambles of rumination and negativity.

Your constant inner dialog distracts you from what is happening around you, right here and now. It causes you to miss valuable experiences and sabotages the joy of the present moment.

Absurdly, we assume we need to think more or harder in order to "figure out" why we aren't as happy or fulfilled as we wish we could be. We try to pinpoint the possessions, people, and experiences that might quench our longings and ease our unhappiness. The more we ponder our despair, the more despondent we become. Our thoughts make us restless, empty, and agitated as we project into the future or look to the past for answers.

In fact, nearly every negative thought you have relates to the past or future. It's common to find yourself trapped in a looping cycle of regretful thinking or worry thoughts, even while feeling desperate to escape the never-ending tape playing in your mind.

Not only do you struggle with your thoughts, but you also struggle with your inability to be free of them. The longer the negative thoughts continue to loop, the worse you feel. It's almost as if there were two of you—the thinker and the judge, the person thinking the thoughts and the person aware that you are thinking them and judging how bad they are.

This thinking/judging dynamic infects us with painful emotions. The more fearful, guilt-ridden, regretful thoughts we have, the more stressed, anxious, depressed, and angry we feel. Sometimes our thoughts paralyze us with bad feelings, and it's those feelings that rob us of inner peace and contentment.

Although our thoughts are the culprit responsible for so much distress, we assume there's not much to be done about it. You can't stop your mind from thinking, right? You can't shut off your brain at will or rid yourself of the mental chatter and associated feelings that prevent you from enjoying life fully.

Occasionally, we have unexpected moments of mental peace and quiet. More often, however, we try to quell the mental chatter by self-medicating with too much food, alcohol, drugs, work, sex, or exercise. But these are temporary solutions to muffle the noise and ease the pain. Soon enough, our thoughts are back at it again, and the cycle continues.

Are we destined to be victims of our "monkey minds" at all times? Must we constantly battle our thoughts and allow them to drag us down with worry, regret, and anxiety? Is there a way to have a clear mind, free of negativity and pain?

You may not be able to keep your mental house free from clutter all the time, but you can impact your thoughts enough to improve your quality of life and overall happiness in a profound way. Thinking may seem automatic and uncontrollable, but many of our thought patterns are habitual and, well, thoughtless.

Although it appears you and your thoughts are inseparable, you do possess a "conscious self" that can step in with intention and manage your thoughts. You have far more control of your thoughts than you think. When you learn how to control your mind, you open a door to the vastness of creativity, inspiration, and brilliance that is just behind the clutter of those untamed thoughts.

Through various mindfulness practices and practical habits, you can disempower your thoughts and have more "space" in your mind to enjoy inner peace and happiness. You'll have the clarity to prioritize what's most important in your life, what no longer serves your goals, and how you want to live on a daily basis.

Introducing: *Declutter Your Mind*

The goal of this book is simple: We will teach you the habits, actions, and mindsets you can use to clean up the mental clutter that might be holding you back from being more focused and mindful.

Instead of just telling you to do something, we show you how practical, science-backed actions can create real and lasting change if practiced regularly.

Declutter Your Mind is broken down into four information-packed sections that you can use to change a specific aspect of your life that might be causing you to feel stressed or overwhelmed. Specifically, we cover these topics:

1. Decluttering Your Thoughts
2. Decluttering Your Life Obligations

3. Decluttering your Relationships
4. Decluttering Your Surroundings

You'll find that this book is full of exercises that can have an immediate, positive impact on your mindset. Since there is a lot of material, we suggest you read it all the way through one time and then go through it again to identify the one area of your life that needs the most work. In other words, you should find a "quick win" that will have an immediate impact on your life.

Who Are We?

Barrie is the founder of the award-winning personal development site, *Live Bold and Bloom.* She is a certified personal coach and online course creator, helping people apply practical strategies to push past comfort zones and create happier, richer, more successful lives. She is also the author of a series of self-improvement books on positive habits, life passion, confidence building, mindfulness, and simplicity.

As an entrepreneur, a mom of three, and a homeowner, Barrie knows firsthand how valuable and life-changing it is to simplify and manage both our inner and outer lives in order to reduce stress and enjoy life to the fullest.

Steve (or "S.J.") runs the blog Develop Good Habits and is the author of a series of habit-related titles, all of which are available on Amazon at HabitBooks.com. The goal of his content is to show how continuous habit development can lead to a better life.

Together, we are the authors of two previous books about mindfulness and leading a less complicated lifestyle: *10-Minute Declutter: The Stress Free Habit for Simplifying Your Home* and *10-Minute Digital Declutter: The Simple Habit to Eliminate Technology Overload.* Not only do these books teach practical actions to control your material possessions, they also show how eliminating the "noise" in your life can have a positive impact on mental health.

Both of us have different reasons for not only adopting the following principles, but also deciding to write this book in the first place.

Barrie's Story...

Over the last few years, Barrie has had a profound shift in her lifestyle and life priorities. Feeling an emptiness in her life and often dealing with generalized anxiety, she began a personal quest to find what she felt passionate about beyond her role as a mom, and to figure out how to quiet the "voice in her head" that triggered the anxiety and suffering she experienced.

Her journey led her to a new career as a personal coach, personal development blogger, teacher, and author. Through her work and research, she encountered several profound "aha" moments when she learned more about mindfulness practices, simplifying, and identifying a few life priorities where she wanted to spend most of her time and energy.

She recently moved from a congested and busy suburb of Atlanta to Asheville, NC, where she enjoys a slower pace of life in a town that focuses on healthy living, great food, interpersonal connections, nature, and music.

She downsized to a much smaller house, getting rid of many of her possessions and streamlining her wardrobe. She prioritizes relationships, experiences, and meaningful work over things, money, and prestige. In her daily life, she tries to focus on balance and being present, using meditation, exercise, and time in nature as her tools.

Steve's Story...

For many years, Steve led a pretty simplistic lifestyle, but since the second half of 2015 he has experienced **four major life event changes** (marriage, a new baby, buying a house, and starting a brand new business). While all of these events have been amazing, they have also led to an increased amount of stress in his life.

At first, Steve felt overwhelmed by these changes, but he eventually learned how to simplify what goes through his head, and to be in the moment with whatever he is doing at the time. So now, when he spends time with this wife and son, he is 100 percent in the moment; and when he's working, he completes important tasks in a productive flow state.

The strategies that Steve and Barrie both use to overcome the stress in their lives aren't easy. But they definitely work—if you're willing to work at it on a daily basis. These are the strategies that you'll discover in the following book.

Why You NEED to Read *Declutter Your Mind*

This book is for anyone who recognizes how their untamed thoughts are interfering with their focus, productivity, happiness, and peace of mind.

- *Declutter Your Mind* will be a good fit if you:
- Often find yourself trapped in anxious, negative, and unproductive thinking
- Lose valuable time, focus, and energy because of overthinking and worry
- Feel frustrated and confused about how to stop negative and compulsive thinking
- Have experienced times of high stress, agitation, anxiety, and even depression as a result of mental overwhelm
- Find yourself looking to money, possessions, work, success, or prestige to fill a void of emptiness or sadness you feel
- Feel so busy, overwhelmed, and stressed that you've lost touch with who you really are
- Find yourself turning to distractions, alcohol, drugs, and other compulsions to numb yourself to painful thoughts and feelings
- Would like to change your priorities and learn to manage and understand your thoughts so they don't rule your life
- Get complaints from your boss, spouse, or family members about your distraction, disengagement, agitation, or constant stress
- Simply desire a more centered, calm, and peaceful lifestyle

The bottom line?

If you desire to have a simplified, calm mental life—and to reclaim some of the time and emotional energy you give up to overthinking and anxiety—then you've come to the right place. Throughout this book, you will not only learn the skills you need to declutter and manage your thoughts, but also discover actionable strategies to implement immediately.

We have a lot of ground to cover, so let's jump in and discuss why we are so trapped by our thoughts, and how it's impacting us.

Part I

DECLUTTERING YOUR THOUGHTS

Four Causes of Mental Clutter

"It's not a daily increase, but a daily decrease. Hack away at the inessentials."

– Bruce Lee

Before we dive into the various exercises to eliminate your negative thinking, it's important to first understand why you have these thoughts. So, in this section, we'll go over four causes of mental clutter.

Cause #1: Daily Stress

An excessive amount of stress is the primary reason many people feel overwhelmed by life. In fact, the stress created by information overload, physical clutter, and the endless choices required from these things can trigger an array of mental health issues like generalized anxiety, panic attacks, and depression.

Couple this stress with the legitimate worries and concerns in your life, and you may find yourself with sleep problems, muscle pain, headaches, chest pain, frequent infections, and stomach and intestinal disorders, according to the American Psychological Association (not to mention dozens of studies supporting the connection between stress and physical problems).

Dan Harris, ABC News anchor and author of the book 10% Happier, didn't acknowledge how the stress of mental overload was impacting him until he had a full-blown panic attack on national television.

His demanding and competitive job (which took him to the front lines of Afghanistan, Israel, Palestine, and Iraq) had left him depressed and anxious. He self-medicated his internal pain with recreational drugs, triggering the on-air attack.

After a meeting with his doctor, Dan had a wake-up call about his mental state. He says in a post on the ABC website, "As I sat there in his office, the sheer enormity of my mindlessness started to sink in—from hurtling headlong into war zones without considering the psychological consequences, to using drugs for a synthetic squirt of replacement adrenaline. It was as if I had been sleepwalking through a cascade of moronic behavior."

Dan's "moronic behavior" was simply a human reaction to everything that was happening in his head. When life becomes so intense and complicated, our psyches search out escape ramps. Too much input, too much negative exposure, and too many choices can trigger a not-so-healthy coping response.

Cause #2: The Paradox of Choice

The freedom of choice, something revered in free societies, can have a diminishing point of return when it comes to mental health. Psychologist Barry Schwartz coined the phrase "paradox of choice," which sums up his findings that increased choice leads to greater anxiety, indecision, paralysis, and dissatisfaction. More choices might afford objectively better results, but they won't make you happy.

Consider a simple trip to the grocery store. According to the Food Marketing Institute, in 2014 there were 42,214 items carried in the average supermarket. What once might have been a 10-minute excursion to grab the necessities now requires at least that much time to agonize over the best brand of yogurt or the right gluten-free crackers.

Try to purchase a pair of jeans, the staple of most wardrobes, and you'll be faced with an endless array of decisions. Baggy fit? Boot cut? Skinny? Wide leg? Vintage wash? Button fly? Zipper? A simple purchase is enough to make you hyperventilate.

Steve Jobs, Mark Zuckerberg, and even President Obama made the decision to limit their clothing options to minimize feelings of overwhelm from making decisions. In an article from Michael Lewis for Vanity Fair, the president explained the logic behind his limited wardrobe selections:

"You'll see I wear only gray or blue suits," Obama said. "I'm trying to pare down decisions. I don't want to make decisions about what I'm eating or wearing. Because I have too many other decisions to make."

Cause #3: Too Much "Stuff"

Our homes are filled with clothes we never wear, books we won't read, toys that are unused, and gadgets that don't see the light of day. Our computer inboxes are overflowing. Our desktops are cluttered, and our phones are flashing messages like "You need more storage."

As mentioned in 10-Minute Digital Declutter, "We have become such slaves to our gadgets that we'd rather have the quick fix of instant information or entertainment over real-world interactions and experiences."

With this constant flow of information and access to technology, becoming mass consumers of things and data is easier than ever. At the click of a button, we can order anything from a book to a motorboat and have it delivered to our doorstep.

We're filling our homes with things we don't need and filling our time with a steady stream of tweets, updates, articles, blog posts, and cat videos. Information and stuff is piling up around us, and yet we feel helpless to do anything about it.

All of this extraneous stuff and data not only sucks our time and productivity, but also produces reactive, anxious, and negative thoughts.

Like:

- "My Facebook friend looks like she's living a happy life. My life sucks."
- "Should I buy that FitBit and start tracking my health so I don't die too early?"
- "Oh no, I forgot that 'How to Make a Million Before You're 30' webinar—what if they shared something really important?"

Everything seems important <u>and</u> urgent. Every email and text must be answered. Every latest device or contraption must be purchased. This keeps us constantly stirred up, busy with trivialities, and detached from the people around us and the feelings within us.

We often feel like we don't have time to declutter because we're too busy consuming new stuff and information. But at some point, all this busyness is leading us to mental and emotional exhaustion. As we process everything coming at us, we analyze, ruminate, and worry ourselves to the breaking point.

How have we lost sight of the values and life priorities that once kept us balanced and sane? What can we do about it? We can't go back in time and live without technology. We can't renounce all of our worldly possessions and dwell in a cave. We have to figure out a way to live in this modern world without losing our sanity.

Decluttering our stuff and cutting back on time spent with our digital devices does help eliminate some of the anxiety and negative thinking. But we still have plenty of reason to get lost in the mental clutter of negative thinking, worry, and regret.

We worry about our health, our jobs, our kids, the economy, our relationships, how we look, what other people think of us, terrorism, politics, pain from the past, and our unpredictable futures. Our thoughts about these things make us suffer and undermine the happiness we could experience right now if we didn't have that constant voice in our heads stirring things up.

Cause #4: The Negativity Bias

"But it was in this moment, lying in bed late at night, that I first realized that the voice in my head—the running commentary that had dominated my field of consciousness since I could remember—was kind of an asshole." – Dan Harris

The human nervous system has been evolving for 600 million years, but it still responds the same as our early human ancestors who faced life-threatening situations many times a day and simply needed to survive.

Dr. Rick Hanson, Senior Fellow of the Greater Good Science Center at UC Berkeley, in an article on his website says, *"To keep our ancestors alive, Mother Nature evolved a brain that routinely tricked them into making three mistakes: overestimating threats, underestimating opportunities, and underestimating resources (for dealing with threats and fulfilling opportunities)."*

Thus evolved the "negativity bias," our tendency to react to negative stimuli more intensely than positive. Negative stimuli produce more neural activity than do equally intense (e.g., loud, bright) positive ones. They are also perceived more easily and quickly. Hanson says, *"The brain is like Velcro for negative experiences but Teflon for positive ones."*

So what does the negativity bias have to do with your thoughts? It means that you are hardwired to overthink, worry, and view situations more negatively than they are in reality. You see threats as more threatening and challenges as more challenging.

Any negative thought that enters your mind feels real, so there is an impulse to accept it as reality. But you are not living in a cave, facing life-threatening situations daily. You may be hardwired to think negatively, but you don't have to accept this predisposition.

Sam Harris says, *"There is an alternative to simply identifying with the next thought that pops into consciousness."* **That alternative is mindfulness.** Mindfulness can be practiced in the most mundane activities, and it can be fostered through specific exercises that are provided throughout this book.

Mindfulness requires retraining your brain to stay out of the mental clutter from the future and focus instead on the present moment. When you are mindful, you no longer attach to your thoughts. You are simply present in whatever you happen to be doing.

Sounds simple, right?

The concept is deceptively simple—but changing your thinking is not so easy.

As with building any other habit, decluttering your mind requires practice, patience, and a willingness to start small, then grow from there. Fortunately, we'll show how to do all of this throughout this book.

Not only will you learn the practices to train your brain and control your thoughts, but you'll also build the specific habits that will support these mental practices on a daily basis.

In the remainder of this section, we'll go over **four habits you can use to declutter your thoughts**. You'll find that, as you master your thinking, you'll not only be more focused and productive, but also feel more at peace with all the crazy demands of modern life.

So let's dive into the first habit that will retrain your brain—focused breathing.

Mental Declutter Habit #1: Focused Deep Breathing

"Feelings come and go like clouds in a windy sky. Conscious breathing is my anchor."

– Thích Nhat Hanh

Even though you take about 20,000 breaths a day, you probably don't think about your breathing very often. Your brain adjusts your breathing to the needs of your body automatically. When you're climbing stairs or going for a run, you don't have to think, *"I better breathe deeper and harder to get more oxygen to my muscles."* It just happens.

To adjust your breathing to your body's changing needs, sensors in your brain, blood vessels, muscles, and lungs handle the job for you. However, whenever you want to take over, you have that power. You can slow down your breathing, change where you breathe from (chest or abdomen), and even make your breaths shallow or deep.

A change in breathing is often the first sign that our thoughts are overwhelming and stressful. When we feel anxious, depressed, rushed, or upset, we may experience rapid breathing or shortness of breath. Our modern lifestyles and job settings also contribute to improper, shallow breathing.

As Barrie writes in her book *Peace of Mindfulness: Everyday Rituals to Conquer Anxiety and Claim Unlimited Inner Peace*:

> Unfortunately, we are sedentary most of the day, so there is less need to breathe deeply, the way our ancestors did in order to hunt, gather, farm, and perform other manual labor. Sitting behind our desks or slumped on the couch watching TV, we have developed a habit of short and shallow breathing.
>
> When we're in a hurry and rushed, our breathing follows suit with quick, nervous breaths. When we're stressed, anxious, or

focused on a problem, our bodies contract, and we bend forward, with our heads down, arms together, and muscles tensed.

All of these postures constrict breathing. Sometimes when we're absorbed with stress and worry, the muscles that move the thorax and control inhalation and muscular tenseness clamp down like a vice to restrict exhalation, and we forget to breathe altogether.

You may not pay much attention to your breathing and your posture, but by simply becoming more aware of how you breathe, you foster a calmer state of body and mind.

Start paying attention to your breathing and simply become aware of how you are taking in and releasing air throughout your day.

We recommend keeping four things in mind while building the focused deep breathing habit:

1. Rather than slouching at your desk or on the sofa at home, sit up straighter to allow more room for your lungs to take in oxygen. Become aware of areas where your body is tense, and mentally "breathe into" those areas, seeing them relax as you breathe.

2. Be conscious of breathing through your nose rather than your mouth. Your nose has defense mechanisms that prevent impurities and excessively cold air from entering your body. Your nose also can detect poisonous gases that could be harmful to you. Viruses and bacteria can enter the lungs through mouth breathing, so let your nose do the work.

3. When you inhale, use abdominal breathing by gently pushing your stomach outward, and breathe through as though you're filling your stomach. On the exhale, breathe out slowly and allow your stomach to return to its normal position.

4. Pay attention to the difference between shallow breathing (which stops at the chest) and abdominal or diaphragmatic breathing (which fills the lower lobes of the lungs and encourages full oxygen exchange). Abdominal breathing also massages the abdominal organs through the movements of the diaphragm.

One of the best ways to detach from negative thoughts and gain control over your mind is through slow, deep, rhythmic breathing. This focused breathing stimulates the parasympathetic nervous system, reducing your heart rate, relaxing muscles, calming the mind, and normalizing brain function.

Deep breathing helps you feel connected to your body, shifting your awareness away from worry and quieting the inner dialog in your brain. The physiological changes that occur with deep breathing are referred to as the "**relaxation response.**"

The relaxation response is a term first coined by Dr. Herbert Benson, professor, author, cardiologist, and founder of Harvard's Mind/Body Medical Institute. He wrote the book *The Relaxation Response*, in which he shares the benefits of a variety of relaxation techniques (including diaphragmatic breathing) in treating a wide range of stress-related disorders.

Benson says, "The relaxation response is a physical state of deep rest that changes the physical and emotional responses to stress...and the opposite of the fight or flight response."

In addition to promoting the relaxation response, deep breathing has many well-researched health benefits. Here's a summary of what deep nose breathing can do for you:

- Boost nitric oxide, a powerful immune-boosting molecule produced in the sinuses during nose breathing.
- Improve the quality of your blood through eliminating toxins and increased oxygenation.
- Assist the digestion and assimilation of food through a more efficient stomach and digestive system.
- Increase the health and function of the nervous system by increased oxygenation.
- Improve the function of the abdominal organs and the heart through increased circulation.
- Help prevent respiratory problems as the lungs become stronger and more powerful.

- Reduce blood pressure and help prevent heart disease as the heart becomes more efficient and stronger and the workload on the heart is reduced.

- Assist in weight control as extra oxygen burns excess fat more efficiently.

By practicing a few minutes of deep abdominal breathing every day, you are building a life-long habit proven through years of research and testing to clear your mind, reduce stress, and promote relaxation of the mind and body.

Barrie likes to practice deep breathing several times a day when she takes a break from work and before bed to prepare her mind and body for sleep. You can practice mindful breathing just about anywhere at any time of day, especially when you find yourself overthinking or feeling stressed and anxious. Even a few minutes of mindful breathing a day can improve your sense of well-being and mental calm.

However, you might want to develop a regular practice of deep breathing at a specific time of day, as focused breathing is the foundation for a meditation practice, which we'll discuss in the next chapter. **If you establish a 5 – to 10-minute breathing habit, you can easily use this habit as a trigger and starting point for your meditation practice.**

Here is a **seven-step process** you can use to develop the practice of deep breathing on a daily basis:

1. Determine a time of day to practice deep breathing, preferably after a daily habit you perform consistently, like brushing your teeth.

   Morning is always a good time to practice, as it sets the tone for your day. However, you may find you want to take a break in the middle of the day, as things get more hectic during your workday. Before bed is another good time, as it promotes a restful state before sleep.

2. Select a setting for your breathing practice in a quiet space where you won't be distracted or interrupted. Turn off your phone, computer, and any other device that might disturb you.

3. Set a timer for 10 minutes.

4. Sit on the floor with a pillow in a meditative position, like the lotus position, or in a chair with your spine straight and feet planted on the floor. Let your hands rest gently in your lap.

5. Inhale slowly through your nose until your lungs are filled to capacity, allowing your stomach to push out on the inhalation.

6. At the end of the inhalation, pause for a count of two.

7. Exhale slowly, smoothly, and completely, allowing your stomach to return to its natural position. Pause at the end of the exhalation as well.

When you first begin, don't take in too much air in one breath. Start by breathing to the count of four, pausing for the count of two, and exhaling to the count of four. If you notice you're hyperventilating, don't breathe in quite as deeply. With practice, you'll enlarge your lung capacity and can inhale more air.

Now let's move on to another mindfulness practice that involves focused breathing but takes you to another level of calm, mental clarity, and inner peace.

Mental Declutter Habit #2: Meditation

"Meditation is not a way of making your mind quiet. It's a way of entering into the quiet that's already there—buried under the 50,000 thoughts the average person thinks every day." – Deepak Chopra

You don't have to be a Buddhist, a mystic, or a crystal-carrying ex-hippie to practice meditation. You can belong to any spiritual or religious faith or have no religious affiliation at all to reap the benefits of meditation and use it as a tool for decluttering your mind.

If you've never practiced meditation or you're not familiar with it, you might be put off by the idea of sitting quietly in the lotus position and emptying your mind. But don't let the clichés about meditating cave dwellers prevent you from giving it a try.

In his book *10% Happier*, Dan Harris says, "Meditation suffers from a towering PR problem....If you can get past the cultural baggage, though, what you'll find is that meditation is simply exercise for your brain."

Meditation has been practiced for thousands of years and originates in ancient Buddhist, Hindu, and Chinese traditions. **There are dozens of styles of meditative practices, but most practices begin with the same steps—sitting quietly, focusing attention on your breath, and dismissing any distractions that come your way.**

The goal of meditation varies depending on the type of meditation practice and the desired outcome of the meditator. For our purposes here, **we suggest meditation as a tool to help you train your mind and control your thoughts,** both when you are sitting in meditation and when you aren't.

The benefits of meditating translate to your daily life, helping you control worry and overthinking, and providing a host of health benefits that we'll discuss below.

The key to finding satisfaction with meditation is simply to practice. By making a daily commitment to meditation, you will improve your skills and discover how the mental, physical, and emotional benefits increase over time.

Barrie has noticed that, on the days she meditates, she is less anxious and agitated and more focused in her work, especially with writing. She has also noticed an increased ability to stay in the present moment and redirect herself back to the task at hand whenever she feels tempted by a potential distraction. Finally, Barrie uses short meditation breaks during the day to help her relax during particularly stressful times.

The steps to meditating are simple and straightforward, but the practice is not as easy as it seems. You'll discover that, at first, trying to quiet your mind and maintain focus is like attempting to train fleas. But the more you practice, the easier and more enjoyable the experience becomes.

As professor David Levy describes it to *USA Today*, "Meditation is a lot like doing reps at a gym. It strengthens your attention muscle."

Of all of the strategies outlined in this book, meditation is the one that can have the most profound impact on your overall well-being. Meditation has long been touted as a way to improve concentration and focus, but only recently have studies confirmed these claims.

- A study from the University of Washington showed that meditation increases productivity and promotes focus.
- Another study published in *Brain Research Bulletin* supports the claims that meditation can decrease stress.
- A University of Massachusetts Medical School study has shown meditation can boost your overall brainpower in a number of ways.
- Other studies have shown how meditation can help preserve the aging brain, improve the symptoms of depression and anxiety, thicken the learning and memory areas of the brain, and help with addiction.

- Research has found that meditation also promotes divergent thinking, a type of thinking that fosters creativity by allowing many new ideas to be generated.

Our main point in sharing this research is to reinforce the profound benefits of meditation—benefits not only demonstrated by thousands of years of anecdotal evidence, but also validated by solid scientific research. If you have any doubt that meditation is worth your time and effort, hopefully you're beginning to shift your opinion.

Let's get started with the very simple 10-minute meditation Barrie and Steve practice that you can begin today. There isn't anything fancy or complicated about the practice. You don't need special clothes or equipment. All you need is a quiet space and the willingness to stick to it.

Here is a simple 11-step process you can use to build the meditation habit:

1. Select a quiet, calm space for your meditation practice where you can close the door to be completely alone.

2. Determine a specific time of day for your practice. If you've begun a deep breathing practice, you can use this as your trigger (and starting point) for your new meditation habit. Or you can choose another trigger and practice meditating at another time of day.

3. Decide whether you want to meditate sitting on a pillow on the floor or in a straight-back chair or sofa. Try not to recline as you meditate, since you might fall asleep.

4. Remove all distractions and turn off all digital devices or other devices that make noise. Remove pets from the room.

5. Set a timer for 10 minutes.

6. Sit comfortably either in a chair or cross-legged on the floor with a cushion. Keep your spine erect and your hands resting gently in your lap.

7. Close your eyes, or keep them open with a downward-focused gaze, then take a few deep cleansing breaths through your nose—we recommend three or four breaths at a time.

8. Gradually become aware of your breathing. Notice the air moving in and out through your nostrils and the rise and fall of your chest and abdomen. Allow your breaths to come naturally, without forcing them.

9. Focus your attention on the sensation of breathing, perhaps even mentally thinking the word "in" as you inhale and "out" as you exhale.

10. Your thoughts will wander a lot in the beginning. Every time they do, gently let them go and then return your attention to the sensation of breathing.

    Don't judge yourself for having intrusive thoughts. That's just your "monkey mind" trying to take over. Just lead your mind back to focused attention on breathing. You may have to do this dozens of times at first.

11. As you focus on breathing, you'll likely notice other perceptions and sensations like sounds, physical discomfort, emotions, etc. Simply notice these as they arise in your awareness, and then gently return to the sensation of breathing.

Your goal is to increasingly become the witness to all sounds, sensations, emotions, and thoughts as they arise and pass away. View them as though you are observing them from a distance without judgment or internal comment.

Rather than your mind taking control and running away whenever a thought or distraction occurs, you eventually gain more and more control of your mind and your ability to redirect it back to the present.

In the beginning, you'll feel you're in a constant battle with your monkey mind. But with practice you won't need to constantly redirect your thoughts. Thoughts begin to drop away naturally, and your mind opens up to the immense stillness and vastness of just being present. This is a deeply peaceful, satisfying experience.

Meditation masters refer to this space of stillness as the "gap"—the silent space between thoughts. At first the gap is very narrow, and it's difficult to remain there for more than a few nanoseconds. As you become a more practiced meditator, you'll find the gap opens wider and more frequently, and you can rest in it for longer periods of time.

You can experience a brief moment of the space between thoughts by trying this exercise: Close your eyes and begin to notice your thoughts. Simply watch them come and go for a few seconds. Then ask yourself the question, "Where will my next thought come from?" Stop and wait for the answer. You may notice there's a short gap in your thinking while you await the answer.

Eckhart Tolle, author of the book *The Power of Now*, suggests this gap experience is like a cat watching a mouse hole. You're awake and waiting, but with no thoughts in that gap.

You can also practice this "space between thoughts" exercise by putting yourself in a state of deep listening. Sit quietly and listen intently, as though you're trying to hear a quiet and distant sound. Again, you are alert, awake, and waiting without the distraction of thought.

You may not experience a gap moment in your early days of meditating. In fact, you may find you are constantly redirecting your thoughts, noticing your physical discomforts, and wondering why you're bothering with this silly practice at all.

You may judge yourself harshly for not "getting it right," or wonder if you are making any progress at all. During meditation, your mind might wander off on a meandering dialog about how you're feeling and how the meditation is going. Or, if you experience a space between thought moment, you might get distracted by the thrill of finally experiencing it.

Your job is always to simply observe and redirect your mind back to the present moment, to your breathing. The goal of your meditation practice is not to reach nirvana or have a spiritual awakening. It's simply to strengthen your control over your mind until your mind gets the message and gives in. The results of your efforts will be a mental house that you control rather than the other way around.

Some beginning meditators prefer to use a guided meditation to help them get the feel for the practice and stay focused. You can find many free guided meditations online, and there are dozens of smartphone apps available.

We recommend three to get started:

1. Buddhify has over 80 custom guided audio meditation tracks on various topics.

2. Omvana, with dozens of guided meditations by very famous authors, teachers, and spiritual celebrities.

3. Headspace has a series of 10-minute guided exercises for your mind.

If you find you enjoy meditating, gradually increase your practice from 10 minutes a day to 30 minutes. Or you can try two 15-minute meditation sessions during different parts of the day.

Steve and Barrie find it's valuable to keep a meditation diary to make notes about your experiences and feelings during meditation. Try to write in it immediately following your meditation so your memory is fresh. Write down how uncomfortable or distracted you felt, and whether or not you felt the "space between thought" for any period of time. Also, write about any changes in your daily mental state—whether you are feeling more or less anxious, stressed, or worried.

Over time, you'll have a document reflecting how you've improved with your practice, as well as how the practice has impacted your overall state of mind.

Now, if meditation isn't your thing, then you might want to consider a different habit where you learn how to reframe the negative thoughts that often pop into your mind. So let's talk about that next.

Mental Declutter Habit #3: Reframe ALL Negative Thoughts

"Whether you think you can or you think you can't, either way, you are right!" – Henry Ford

Our thinking processes are necessary for survival and for competing in a modern world. Critical thinking gives us the ability to solve problems quickly and effectively. Creative thinking allows us to develop original, diverse, and elaborate ideas and connections. But it's the uninvited negative thinking that clutters our minds and often drains our enthusiasm for life.

According to Australian psychologist Dr. Russ Harris, author of *The Happiness Trap: How to Stop Struggling and Start Living,* "Thus, evolution has shaped our brains so that we are hardwired to suffer psychologically: to compare, evaluate, and criticize ourselves, to focus on what we're lacking, to rapidly become dissatisfied with what we have, and to imagine all sorts of frightening scenarios, most of which will never happen. No wonder humans find it hard to be happy!"

Many people go through their entire lives victimized by their negative thoughts. They feel they have no control of what thoughts take up residence in their brains—and worse, they believe the "voices" in their heads that tell them the sky is falling.

While the negativity bias is real, it isn't impervious to your efforts for change and self-awareness. Though it may feel natural to allow your mind to wander into worry and despair, you've reinforced negative thinking by not challenging it, and by accepting your thoughts as your identity. But you have the power to recognize this tendency and change it by **building the reframing habit**.

The first step is to notice your thought patterns and interrupt them before they get out of control.

Here are six strategies you can use throughout your day to break the pattern and begin taming your mind.

Each of these strategies takes just a few minutes to employ.

Strategy #1. Be the Watcher

Start by becoming aware of your thoughts. Separate your "self" from your thoughts, and just observe what is going on in your mind.

The trick here is to do this in an impartial manner where you're *not* judging any particular thought. Simply be conscious of yourself as a detached witness to your thoughts.

This exercise can be done sporadically throughout the day *or* during a meditation session. Observing your thoughts rather than attaching to them disempowers the thoughts and the emotions they foster.

Strategy #2. Name That Thought

Another way to separate yourself from your thoughts is by mentally acknowledging that they are nothing more than thoughts—*not* your reality.

For example, if you think, *"I'll never get all of this done,"* change the mental dialog to *"I'm having the thought that I'll never get all of this done."*

This reinforces the fact that you are not your thoughts.

Strategy #3. Just Say No

When you catch yourself in mental looping or worry, simply say, "STOP!" out loud (vocalizing reinforces the interruption), and then visualize a heavy metal wall slamming down in front of your runaway thoughts.

Barrie sometimes visualizes pushing negative thoughts into a deep hole or putting them into a balloon that floats away.

Strategy #4. Try the Rubber Band Trick

Wear a rubber band on your wrist. Whenever you see it, stop and notice your thoughts. If you are stuck in negative thinking, put the rubber band on the other wrist or gently pop it on your wrist. This physical action interrupts the flow of negative thought.

Strategy #5. Know Your Triggers

Often, overthinking and negativity are triggered by a person, situation, or physical state. Pay attention to common worries and anxieties you brood about.

Is there anything that happens that sets these off in your mind?

If so, write down the triggers so you're aware when they happen. This awareness can help prevent you from being ambushed by negative thoughts.

Strategy #6. Distract Yourself

Break the cycle using distraction. Do something that will occupy your mind so there's no room for the negative thoughts. Immerse yourself in a project that involves focus and brainpower.

If you're stuck in the car or waiting in line, go through the multiplication tables in your head or try to memorize a poem.

Mental Declutter Habit #4: Teach Your Old Mind New Tricks

Truthfully, you will always struggle with some amount of negative thinking. You can't overcome millions of years of evolutionary wiring through sheer willpower. As Dr. Russ Harris says, "Any search for a 'pain-free existence' is doomed to failure."

However, you can manage the pain by being more proactive in what you allow to remain in your thoughts.

Interrupting cluttered thinking is only part of the process of retraining your brain and learning to disassociate from negative thoughts. Your mind abhors a vacuum, **so you need to fill the void with constructive thought so you don't career back into old patterns.**

Here are four ways to do this:

#1. Challenge the Thought and Replace It

You may notice that many of your thoughts are wildly exaggerated. They are not the truth, or at least not the whole truth. You might think, "I'm a loser, I can never do anything right." In the moment, you certainly *feel* like a loser, but if you examine the thought, you recognize that it's not entirely truthful. You've done plenty of things well and have been successful on many occasions.

Rather than allowing "all or nothing" thinking to have a free pass, challenge these negative thoughts whenever they occur. This simply means coming up with a concrete example that contradicts the thought by reminding yourself of a positive event or previous "win."

For instance, let's say you're a writer who receives a negative review on a recent book. Your first thought might be, "I'm a terrible writer—everyone hates what I write." However, if you take the time to look at the 100 previous positive reviews, then you'll recognize that the majority of your readers love your content.

Using positive reminders might feel awkward at first, but eventually you'll train yourself to interrupt those cycles of negative thinking. This habit helps you take control of your reality and puts a roadblock in front of the never-ending highway of self-sabotaging beliefs.

#2 Practice Acceptance

One question you might have is "what do you do about those negative thoughts that are true?" In other words, how do you cope in those times when there is a legitimate reason for having negative thoughts?

The truth is that there are times when you'll feel like it's impossible to maintain a positive outlook. However, it's also true that the *thoughts and feelings* about these challenging situations are often far worse than the situation itself.

You can't completely eradicate your troubled thoughts during hard times, but you can lessen them through acceptance. When you struggle against the reality of a bad situation, you're adding another layer of suffering to your psyche. You can't worry or guilt yourself into a solution. Instead, you need a clear head and a calm mind.

When you find yourself struggling and ruminating, stop for a moment and simply say, "I accept this situation is happening." Take a deep breath and try to stop mentally fighting against it. As you begin to accept this challenge, you can…

- Determine any actions to take to improve or rectify it.
- Seek out anything positive you can learn from it.
- Find ways to get support as you are enduring it.

Acceptance of a situation doesn't mean you avoid action. It means you don't blindly fight and claw to escape. You put yourself in a state of mind that allows you to take correct and useful action.

#3. Take Mindful Action

Overthinking is usually a pointless activity, so why not turn that energy into structured thinking and then action?

When your thoughts are cluttered, do something positive that will distract you from negative thoughts. Just about anything that requires some brain power and focus will do the trick, but we suggest you take mindful action—action that focuses on your values, goals, or priorities.

A quick way to do this is to define your goals, which is something we discuss in the next section. In fact, one of the first mindful actions you could take is to define your values and priorities for the next year.

Some other ideas that you might try include:

- Writing
- Practicing an instrument
- Constructing something by hand
- Painting or drawing
- Working on a complex problem
- Studying
- Memorizing something
- Practicing a speech
- Designing something from scratch

All of these activities require focus and some level of mental challenge, which helps prevent you from falling back into random overthinking or worry.

#4. Set a Worry Timer

You can't completely break the *worry habit*. There will be times when you're flooded with such powerful negative thoughts that no amount of self-talk or distraction works.

But even during these times, you don't have to fall headfirst into the quicksand of negative thinking. You can limit the amount of time you spend in your head so you don't sink so far you can't easily get out.

Set a timer for 10 to 15 minutes and allow yourself to stress over whatever enters your mind. Get it all out! Take this time to express all of the bottled up feelings and thoughts. In fact, during your "worry time," you might even write down your thoughts in a journal. Writing in longhand helps you process your thoughts and can often lead to a creative solution to your problem.

When the timer goes off, get up and do something distracting (as suggested in the previous strategy) to help you taper off of this worry time. If you find one worry session isn't enough, plan for one early in the day and one later in the afternoon. When you start to get back into your head in between sessions, remind yourself to hold off until the next one.

Final Thoughts on Decluttering Your Thoughts

You may not use all of these strategies for training your mind to work more constructively, but they give you an arsenal of tools to choose from so you're prepared. Barrie has found the ability to challenge thoughts and recognize how they don't always reflect reality to be particularly helpful in reducing worry and overthinking.

You'll discover which of these practices work best for you and the mental clutter that often occupies your mind. Don't get discouraged if you find yourself falling back into old patterns. With any new behavior, you have to practice regularly before it becomes more automatic.

Now, let's switch gears by talking about the importance of identifying your "why" and how it can eliminate many of the mental obstacles that occur *and* streamline your life where you focus on what matters most to you.

Part II

DECLUTTERING YOUR LIFE OBLIGATIONS

The Importance of Core Values

One of the challenges of modern living is figuring out *what's truly important* and differentiating those from the obligations that seem important at first, but really don't matter when you take the time to examine them. If you're like most people, then you might find that it's increasingly difficult to minimize, organize, or bypass the deluge of information you encounter on a regular basis.

Today, we have more information, data, and material possessions available to us than any previous generation, but this new way of life doesn't come with instructions on how to manage it all.

Many of us feel so overwhelmed that we fail to step back and assess the impact of information overload. Nor do we know how to prioritize it all. We become reactors to what life throws at us, rather than carefully evaluating what is *best* for us.

Our grandparents and great-grandparents were certainly as busy as we are. They didn't have the benefit of all of the time-saving technology to make their lives easier and more productive. But they did have one big advantage over our generation—they weren't inundated with the stream of information and deluge of choices that we experience every minute of the day.

They were clear on how to prioritize their time, with less money and fewer choices to entice or confuse them. The "Greatest Generation," those who grew up during the Great Depression, had strong, clear values and priorities, and a solid sense of purpose forged during the difficult years during and after World War II.

A strong work ethic coupled with a focus on family, faith, and patriotism defined this generation of Americans. They knew who they were and what they stood for, and therefore how to focus their time and energy.

Fortunately, there is actually a simple solution to cutting through the "noise" of modern society, which can help you make effective decisions whenever you feel overwhelmed by all the available options: **Define your core values**.

Why Core Values?

One of the simplest ways to eliminate mental clutter and live a more fulfilling life is to define *your* values and guiding principles for your life. Now, more than ever, we need these principles to help us clarify how we want to spend our time, energy, and money.

Why is this important?

Because your core values can serve as a measuring stick for all of your choices and decisions in life, keeping you focused on the person you want to be and the life you wish to lead. By living in alignment with your values, you create the best environment for happiness, inner peace, and clear thinking.

Core values form a foundation for your life that endures through time, life difficulties, and major changes. Embracing your core values is like being a tree with deep and stable roots—the storms of life will not dislodge you. When you're clear on your values, you reduce confusion, overthinking, worry, and anxiety.

For example, one of Barrie's core values in her professional life is freedom and flexibility. Once she defined this value, she didn't want to pursue a traditional 9-to-5 job because she knew she wouldn't be happy. Even when great job opportunities came her way, it was easy to say, "No, thank you," because she was clear on her values.

Personal development blogger and author Steve Pavlina describes the importance of core values like this:

> Values act as our compass to put us back on course every single day, so that day after day, we're moving in the direction that takes us closer and closer to our definition of the "best" life we could possibly live. The "best" is your own ideal, but generally as you get closer to this ideal, you'll enjoy increasingly positive shades of "better" even if you never reach "best." And this makes sense because many results in life exist on a continuum.

Living out of alignment with your values or outgrowing your existing values can throw you off course and contribute to feelings of anxiety and depression. If you haven't defined your values, your life can feel unbalanced or directionless, and you may not know why.

In this section, we go over four strategies to define your core values and make intelligent decisions about your life obligations, so what you do on a daily basis matches up with these important items.

Strategy #1: Identify YOUR Core Values

To understand why something feels wrong, you must have a strong grasp of what is right for you.

Who do you want to be and how do you want to live your life?

If you have never defined your values, you are sailing the sea of life without a compass. You're allowing the winds and storms to define your direction and accepting the outcome without question. Even if you have defined them in the past, it doesn't hurt to revisit them, as your values can change over time.

Here's a six-step process for defining your values.

1. First, go through this list of value words (page 138), and write down every value word that feels important to you for your personal life.

2. Then, go through the list again, and write down every value word that feels important for your career or business.

3. For both lists, pick your top five to six values, and write them down on two separate sheets of paper. Title one sheet "Life Values" and the other "Work Values.

4. Under each value, list all of the ways you are currently living out of alignment with this value. For example, if one of your values is quality time with family, but you travel five days a week, you may not be honoring this value.

5. For each value, think about actions you could take to fix those out-of-alignment situations. Ask yourself, "What do I need to do to correct this situation so I'm honoring my core values?"

   If you use the example about family time, maybe one action is cutting back on your travel schedule, or hiring out some household tasks when you're home so you can spend more quality time with family. Write these down for both life and work even if the actions seem impossible right now.

6. On both lists of actions, put a check mark next to the actions that are doable for you now or in the near future. Break these actions down into even smaller, easily manageable actions. These actions might involve making calls, rearranging your schedule, delegating some responsibilities, brainstorming a possible career change, thinking of ways to reengage with your spouse, etc.

Once you have a list of values that align with your goals, review it on a daily basis and make sure that the actions you take match these desired outcomes. You may want to focus first on your personal values and then on your professional values. Or you might choose one value from each and start there.

No matter what you pick, be sure to start with the area of your life where you feel the biggest disconnect. This is where you likely feel the most internal pain and mental agitation. Chip away at your action list daily so you can create changes and boundaries that prevent you from mindlessly wandering away from your values again.

Even small, incremental changes can create a huge, positive shift in your attitude. You'll have a sense of direction and a purpose that feels authentic to you, even if you can't act on it all immediately. This is an incredibly empowering feeling!

You'll still have times of transition and upheaval, but this values exercise gives you the tools to navigate through all of life's ups and downs.

Strategy #2: Clarify Your Life Priorities

Once you've defined your core values, you should use this information to complete another exercise that will enrich your life—**clarify your life priorities so you know exactly how you want to spend your time, energy, and money.**

Without knowing our priorities, we allow the pressures of life to determine our actions and decisions. An email comes in, and we respond. An enticing offer appears on our Facebook page, and we buy it. Someone interrupts our work flow, and we allow it. When we don't know the bigger "why" of our lives, there are no rules, no boundaries, no priorities to help us.

Here's another exercise that we recommend that will help you figure out where you are currently spending your time, energy, and money.

Answer the following questions as honestly as possible. (Also, be sure to have your list of personal and professional core values handy as you answer.)

- How much time per day do you feel you waste on activities unrelated to your core values (i.e., surfing the net, watching mindless TV, shopping, or working in a job you hate)?
- How are you spending money unconsciously?
- How are you interacting with the people you care about unconsciously?
- How do you make career decisions (i.e., do you have a predetermined plan or do you spend most of your day in "reaction mode")?
- How much time do you spend worrying about how you should best spend your time and money?
- What tasks, obligations, and relationships are you allowing in your life unconsciously?

- How are you neglecting other important parts of your life that you never seem to have time for?

Now that you see how you're actually spending your energy and focus, let's determine the ideal way you'd like to prioritize the important areas of your life.

For the sake of this discussion, let's look at **seven main life areas** to help you establish your priorities and how you want to spend your time and money.

If you want to add or remove any of these areas, feel free to do so if they don't apply to you now.

The areas are:

1. Career
2. Family
3. Marriage (or love partnership)
4. Spiritual/personal growth/self-improvement
5. Leisure/social
6. Life management (i.e., home tasks, financial planning, budgeting, etc.)
7. Health and fitness

If you sleep 8 hours a day, that leaves 16 waking hours. Let's remove 2 hours a day for personal hygiene activities and eating. That leaves 14 waking hours a day or 98 hours a week. For the sake of simplicity, let's round that up to 100 hours a week.

In an ideal world, how would you prioritize those seven key areas of your life? How many hours of those 100 per week would you prefer to devote to each area (using your values to help guide you)?

Two examples...

Barrie's current life priorities focus heavily on career, love relationship, and life management. Her children are young adults, and since she recently moved to a new city, many of her friends and family aren't nearby.

Ideally, she'd like to give more time to leisure and social activities, as well as fitness and self-improvement. She is trying to focus more on these things as she gets more acclimated to her new location.

Steve's current priority focuses heavily on family, due to his recent marriage, the birth of his son, and the fact that his parents just turned 70. So his current goal is to spend as much time as possible with the people he loves the most in the world.

While his career (i.e., online business) and fitness were the biggest priorities only a few years ago, they now are less important than his interpersonal relationships. Often, this means "letting go" of the major goals that once seemed important. So while he still likes to work hard, he has learned to not feel anxious if he can't hit a milestone related to business or his fitness.

Now, these are just two examples from the authors. To help you find your priorities, we recommend answering two simple questions:

1. How different is your current life priority reality from your ideal?
2. What are some actions you need to take to focus your efforts on what really matters to you?

We recommend you begin with the priority that can make the most positive difference in your life or where you feel the most imbalance. You may find this area reflects one or more of your values that you aren't honoring.

For example, you might have a core value related to family, and a life priority of spending more time with your family. Start small by making the decision to add one extra hour a week spending quality time with your family.

Of course, this will bump out some other activity, but you often bump out something that can be easily bumped out—or at least something that isn't a big priority.

Continue adding weekly time to your life priorities until you have them rearranged to more closely match your ideal.

Sometimes, changing a priority can be difficult. If you want to spend more time with your family, will that impact your work schedule? If so, what do you need to do to manage any fallout?

If you want to focus more on your health and fitness, you'll have to create new and challenging habits to ensure you follow through on this priority.

If you want to have a healthy, happy marriage, you may have to give up time in front of the TV or on the computer, which might be hard at first.

Just stating your life priorities isn't enough. You have to take the sometimes difficult actions necessary to make the changes you want to see in your life. But the closer you come to your ideal, the less internal conflict and struggle you'll feel.

Over time, you won't miss those old habits, choices, and behaviors—and your life will flow more easily because you are living authentically, true to your values and priorities.

Exercise #3a: Focus on Mindful Goal Setting

A natural outcome of having values and setting priorities is considering how these apply to your life in the future. Although worrying about the future contributes to an unsettled mind, *planning* for the future is an important and valuable exercise that can set the stage for true fulfillment in the years to come.

But is it really possible to look toward a better future and *still* be happy with your life right now? Can you be content *and* evolving at the same time? We believe it's possible to focus on the future while still learning how to enjoy the present moment.

There are many great writers and philosophical thinkers who talk about contentedness in the present moment. The renowned psychologist Abraham Maslow reminds us that "the ability to be in the present moment is a major component of mental wellness."

Thích Nhat Hanh, the Zen Buddhist monk and bestselling author, teaches that every moment in your life, every breath, every step you take, should be consciously experienced as a moment of joyous arrival.

He suggests you don't need to wait for change, for something better, for the future, before you are content. You can be content right now if you choose to see all of the good and beauty around you in the present moment.

Of course, *this is easier said than done.*

The realities of our daily lives are constantly pulling us into the future. We worry about paying the bills, how our children will turn out, whether we will remain healthy. And the very nature of setting goals is future-oriented.

Longing and struggling against "what is" causes suffering. Wishing for more, for something different, for something better at the expense of contentment in the moment robs us of life.

If that's the case, why should you focus on your future goals if they pull you away from the moment?

Because change and transformation will happen to you whether or not you decide to focus on it.

Change is a constant of life, whether we are sitting in the lotus position absorbed in the moment or wringing our hands about some imagined future outcome. So we might as well create our futures mindfully.

When you embrace the truth that contentment <u>and</u> change can happen simultaneously, you reduce the tension between thinking it's an either/or proposition. There is a way to establish a balance between mindfulness and self-creation.

You can view *the process* of creating and reaching your goals as a place for happiness and contentment. Rather than holding back happiness while you await an outcome, enjoy every step along the path. Every revelation, every small action toward your goals should be savored and celebrated.

Knowing that goal-setting isn't incompatible with mindfulness, let's discuss how to create and work toward your goals in a way that supports the bigger "why" of your life.

When you first sit down to ponder your goals for the future, remember to have your core values and life priorities handy as points of reference. As long as your values and priorities remain valid, they should be the compass for directing your goals. Otherwise, you set yourself up for a future of frustration and unhappiness.

In the next section, we will go over the process that Steve uses to create simple goals focused on what's truly important. The benefit of this strategy is that you'll feel less stressed about the future, and instead focus on what's currently going on in your life.

Strategy #3b: Create Quarterly S.M.A.R.T. Goals

The simplest way to focus on what's truly important in life is to create S.M.A.R.T. goals that will be achieved in the immediate future. This means you'll set goals for each quarter (i.e., three months) instead of the yearlong goals that often take you out of the present moment.

To begin, let's start with a simple definition of S.M.A.R.T. goals:

George Doran first used the S.M.A.R.T. acronym in the November 1981 issue of the *Management Review*.

It stands for: **S**pecific, **M**easurable, **A**ttainable, **R**elevant, and **T**ime-bound.

Here's how it works:

S: Specific

Specific goals answer your six "W" questions: *who, what, where, when, which, and why.*

When you can identify each element, you'll know which tools (and actions) are required to reach a goal.

- Who: Who is involved?
- What: What do you want to accomplish?
- Where: Where will you complete the goal?
- When: When do you want to do it?
- Which: Which requirements and constraints might get in your way?
- Why: Why are you doing it?

Specificity is important because, when you reach these milestones (date, location, and objective), you'll know for certain you have achieved your goal.

M: Measurable

Measurable goals are defined with precise times, amounts, or other units—essentially anything that measures progress toward a goal.

Creating measurable goals makes it easy to determine if you have progressed from point A to point B. Measureable goals also help you figure out when you're headed in the right direction, and when you're not. Generally, a measurable goal statement answers questions starting with "how," such as "how much," "how many," and "how fast."

A: Attainable

Attainable goals stretch the limits of what you think is possible. While they're not impossible to complete, they're often challenging and full of obstacles. The key to creating an attainable goal is to look at your current life and set an objective that seems *slightly* beyond your reach. That way, even if you fail, you still accomplish something of significance.

R: Relevant

Relevant goals focus on what you truly desire. They are the exact opposite of inconsistent or scattered goals. They are in harmony with everything that is important in your life, from success in your career to happiness with the people you love.

T: Time-bound

Time-bound goals have specific deadlines. You are expected to achieve your desired outcome before a target date. Time-bound goals are challenging and grounding. You can set your target date for today, or you can set it for a few months, a few weeks, or a few years from now. The key to creating a time-bound goal is to set a deadline you'll meet by working backward and developing habits (more on this later).

S.M.A.R.T. goals are clear and well-defined. There is no doubt about the result you want to achieve. At its deadline, you'll know if you *have* or *haven't* achieved a particular goal.

As an example, here are S.M.A.R.T. goals related to the seven areas of your life that we mentioned in the previous section:

1. Career: "I will acquire five new projects for my Web design consultancy through referrals, networking, and social media marketing campaigns within two months."

2. Family: "I will strengthen my bond with my family by taking them for a vacation at least once in six months. This will be accomplished by setting aside an hour each month during my review session and planning out future trip ideas."

3. Marriage (or love partnership): "I will identify three things I really love about my partner, and tell her about them on Friday night. This will be done by scheduling a 30-minute block on Tuesday so I can reminisce about all the good times we've shared together."

4. Spiritual/personal growth/self-improvement: "I will take five minutes each day to give thanks for everything that's good in my life. I will develop this habit by setting aside time right before my lunch to remember what's important."

5. Leisure/social: "I will dedicate three hours every week to learn and practice watercolor painting. This will be done by eliminating unimportant habits like watching TV."

6. Life management: "I will save 10 percent of every paycheck and invest it in index funds through my 401k."

7. Health and fitness: "I will work out a minimum of 30 minutes per day, three days per week by December 31."

Hopefully, these seven examples give you an idea of how to create S.M.A.R.T. goals that lead to a balanced life. Now let's go over a six-step process that will turn this information into action.

Step #1: Identify What's Important to You

The key to achieving meaningful goals *isn't* to focus on all of the areas of your life. The reason is simple: If you want to find meaning in what you do, then you'll quickly feel overwhelmed if your days are fixated on a laundry list of goals. Yes, it's important to be forward thinking, but you also want enough time to live in the present moment.

Our advice is to **focus on three to four areas of your life**. You can do this by looking at the seven areas we've discussed and identifying what's most important to you right now. From there, simply create goals that tap into an outcome you find both challenging and exciting.

Step #2: Focus on Three-Month Goals

It's been Steve's experience that long-term goals are constantly shifting. What seems urgent today often isn't important next month. So the strategy that works *for him* is to take the major priorities in his life and then break them down into three-month (or quarterly) goals.

Why should you focus on three-month goals?

Because your life is fast-paced and constantly shifting. In order to keep up with all these changes, it's often better to create goals for the short term because this helps maintain consistent effort and a high level of motivation.

It's also been Steve's experience that lengthy goals (i.e., anything over six months) are often *demotivating*. When you know an outcome is months away, it's easy to procrastinate on taking consistent action. You keep putting off your goals, promising you'll work on them *next week*. Next thing you know, it's a year later and nothing has been accomplished.

So to keep things simple, we recommend identifying the three to four areas of your life that are most important to you *right now,* and then creating a specific S.M.A.R.T. goal for each one that you hope to achieve within the next three months.

Step #3: Use a Weekly Review to Create a Schedule

It's *not* always easy to consistently work on your goals when you have a dozen other obligations. Fortunately, there is a simple solution to this dilemma—schedule a weekly review session where you create a daily action plan for the next seven days.

The weekly review is a great concept that David Allen teaches in *Getting Things Done*. It's a simple process. Once a week (Steve prefers Sundays), look at the next seven days and schedule the activities/projects you'd like to accomplish.

You can accomplish all of this with three simple steps:

1. **Answer three questions:** Think carefully about the next seven days and answer these three questions: *What are my personal obligations? What are my priority projects? How much time do I have?*

   Your responses to these questions are extremely important because they will determine the amount of time that can be devoted to your goals during the next seven days.

   The lesson here is that you *shouldn't* schedule your week with hundreds of activities. That's the quickest path to leading a mentally cluttered life. Instead, it's better to recognize, ahead of time, a realistic amount of time that can be dedicated to your important goals.

2. **Schedule project tasks:** After answering these three questions, map out the next seven days. The simplest way to do this is to look at the list for each goal and schedule time to follow-up on the most important activities.

3. **Process captured ideas:** If you're like Barrie and Steve, then you probably have *dozens* of great ideas every week related to your goals. The question is, how do you follow up on them? My advice is to process these notes, making one of two choices: 1) Take action on it immediately or 2) schedule a time when you'll follow up on it. Here's how that would work:

*If the idea is actionable…*then write out a step-by-step plan for how you'll do it. Simply write down a series of actions you'll take on this idea and then schedule these ideas into your week.

*If the idea is NOT actionable…*then put the idea into an archive folder that's reviewed every month. If you do this for every idea you have, you won't forget to follow up at the right time.

The weekly review is an important part of achieving your goals. When you plan out each week, you create a sense of urgency, making it more likely you will follow up on each goal. Your weekly review will also help you create a schedule you can turn into a list of daily activities.

Step #4: Take Action on Your Goals

It's impossible to achieve your goals without action. In fact, the trick to getting what you want is to schedule time into your week that's solely dedicated to your goals. That's why we recommend the following actions:

- **Turn your goal into a project**: The easiest way to do this is to look at the target date and work your way backward. Visualize reaching this milestone. What are the specific steps you completed to get to this point? Once you identify the actions, you simply put them down into a simple, step-by-step list.

- **Schedule time to work on goals**: *How much time* you spend on each goal depends on what's required for each activity. Some tasks might only require a few minutes each week, while others require hours of your day (that's why it's important to understand the time commitment of each goal). Figure out how much time you'll need for each task and schedule them into your week.

- **Turn goals into priority tasks**: We all have those busy schedules full of activities that conflict with one another. The solution? Start your day by working on goals first thing in the morning, or some other time when you feel the most energetic.

- **Schedule time for single actions**: Many people get bogged down by the single actions that are important but not immediately urgent. A quick fix for this is to schedule time each week to complete a number of single actions.

The tool that Steve uses for these single actions is the ToDoist app. Whenever he sets a three-month goal, he creates it as a project in ToDoist and then he adds all the single actions that are required to achieve it. Finally, he schedules specific actions into his weekly calendar.

(For more on how to do this in ToDoist, here is a comprehensive guide they put together that will walk you through the entire process: http://bit.ly/1qMNoh1.)

Step #5: Review Your Goals

The key to achieving anything in life is *consistency*. That's why you should review your "goal project" on a daily basis and make sure you're hitting every important milestone. We recommend creating specific measurements for each step of the process and using a weekly review to make sure you're touching on those as well.

Setting aside time for a daily review is a key step to achieving any goal. It doesn't matter how busy you are—if you are not reviewing your goals every day, you will be less likely to succeed.

The truth is, sometimes life can throw major curveballs in your pursuit of a long-term objective. Often, these challenges can be frustrating and cause you to feel less excited about a goal. So our advice is simple: Review your goals *at least* two to three times per day. That way, you can keep them at the forefront of your mind and remind yourself why you're taking a specific action on a daily basis.

Step #6: Evaluate Your Quarterly Goals

You work hard on your goals every day. You even review them on a weekly and daily basis. The problem? Some people never take a step back and understand the "why" behind each goal. In other words, people don't review their goals to see if they're *actually* worth pursuing. That's why it's important to evaluate your goals every three months, make sure they are aligned with your life purpose, and then create new goals based on what you've learned.

You can complete this evaluation by answering a number of questions:

- Have I attained the desired outcome?
- What were the successful *and* unsuccessful strategies?
- Did I put 100 percent of my effort toward completing these goals? If not, why?
- Have I achieved results consistent with my efforts?
- Should I create a similar goal for the next quarter?
- What goals should I eliminate or alter?
- Is there anything new I'd like to try?

Even though it takes a few hours to complete this evaluation, you should always take time do it every quarter. It will be your ultimate safeguard against wasting time on a goal that *doesn't* align with your long-term plans.

So, that was a brief introduction to the value of setting S.M.A.R.T. goals. Now, the best way to make sure you're actually setting goals that you truly want is to connect them with a personal passion. In the next (and final) strategy we will show you how to do this.

Strategy #4: Connect Goals to Your Passions

Too many people live lives of quiet desperation. They wake up with a low-level sense of dread, anxiety, or sadness. At work, they feel underutilized, unappreciated, and underwhelmed. And when they get home, they feel mentally and physically exhausted, with just enough energy to take care of the kids, fix a meal, and plop onto the couch to watch a few hours of television. Then they wake up and *do it all over again*.

Even if this doesn't describe you exactly, I'm sure you can relate. We *all* get in the occasional rut. We accept less than our dreams. We stay in jobs that don't inspire us or make us happy. All of this angst adds to our mental clutter and distraction.

Life has a way of swallowing us up, and before we know it we're far down a path that feels nothing like who we are or what we want for our lives. By the time we realize it, we have obligations and responsibilities that add yet another reason to stick with the status quo—even if we hate it.

While the concept of "finding your passion" might remind you of those woo-woo quotes you often see on Facebook or Instagram, it still is incredibly important to connect what you do on a daily basis with goals that you feel are truly important.

The reality is that your mental health can be negatively impacted when you feel unfulfilled with your work. Think about how much negative mental energy you've devoted to a bad boss, a job you hate, or a career move you regret. We spend huge chunks of our lives working, so the decision *you* make about your job will have the potential to make or break your overall happiness.

If you find work that you love, you not only free your mind from oppressive thoughts, but will also feel energized in all areas of your life.

So what does it mean to live your passion?

We think it can be defined with a few examples:

- Most days you wake up feeling enthusiastic and happy about what you have going on that day.

- You feel like you're in the "right" place, doing something in your work or life that feels authentic to who you are and how you're wired.

- You attract interesting, like-minded people in your life and work.

- You have a sense of self-confidence and empowerment about what you're doing because it's a great fit for you.

- You experience a deeper purpose or meaning—or at least you are more fulfilled in general.

- Your overall life is better and your relationships are happier because you are more content, self-directed, and present in your work.

Finding your passion and making it part of your life isn't something that happens overnight, and it isn't an exact "paint by numbers process." It's not like teaching you how to follow a recipe or change the oil in your car. It involves a variety of actions and experiments to figure it out. In fact, Barrie teaches the process in her Path to Passion online course, and in her book *The 52-Week Life Passion Project*.

Everyone who reads this book is unique. We all have different personalities, aptitudes, dreams, and life obligations. What *you* determine to be your passion may differ from what others find for themselves. So that's why we recommend a 14-step exercise you can use to find your passion.

Step 1: Write a vision.

Using your values and priorities as guides, write down what you want in every area of your life—especially in your work. You may not know precisely what to include, but a good starting point is to describe what you DON'T want.

For example, when Barrie wrote her life vision five years ago, it looked like this:

I live in an interesting, progressive, vibrant city where I can enjoy nature, the arts, culture, great food, and likeminded people. I'm working in a career I love where I help people, utilizing my coaching and interpersonal skills, as well as my writing and creative skills.

My work is flexible and allows me the freedom to travel and work from anywhere. My income continues to increase, but I do not allow my career to create imbalance in my life.

I am in a relationship that is loving, respectful, and mutually supportive with a smart, creative, funny, kind, and ethical man. I have a network of close and supportive friends and family with whom I regularly spend time, and I have a loving, positive relationship with each of my three young adult children. I frequently spend time in nature, and travel to new locations several times a year. I remain active, energetic, and health conscious with every passing year, and I remain open to new opportunities and possibilities for my life.

She can honestly say that she has made this vision a reality by moving to a new city, building an online business related to personal development and helping others, going on several amazing trips, and nurturing her relationships, health, and freedom.

Our recommendation is to write down what you want and then revise it along the way whenever you recognize something you do/don't want in your life. Finally, post this vision where you can see it every day.

Step 2: Revisit your current life.

If you feel yourself focusing too much on what you *don't like* about your life, then take a look at your current life to see how much of it matches the vision from the previous exercise. You want to maintain those things, and remind yourself that part of your vision is already happening for you...right now!

Write a list of everything in your work that you do enjoy or view as positive—whether it's the comfy desk chair or the client you really like. Write the same list for your personal life, including everything about your life that is working well for you.

Don't throw out the baby with the bath water when you're seeking your passion. Sometimes we overlook positive things in our lives when we're so focused on the negative.

If you want to learn more about this subject, then read this blog post (http://bit.ly/2aHpZGq) on *mindful journaling* that will help you recognize possible passions you might be overlooking right now.

Step 3: Investigate yourself.

Begin learning more about who you are, what motivates you, and what your strengths are. Take some online personality assessments like:

- The Myers Briggs Test
- The Keirsey Temperament Sorter
- Or strengths assessment tests like Strengths Finder 2.0

Learn everything you can about your personality type. You'll find that this information about you gives you a sense of self-awareness that is both comforting and enlightening.

Step 4: Start reading.

Set aside 10 minutes a day to read everything you can about your interests or ideas for potential passions. Look at how other people have translated these interests and ideas into careers. Make notes about anything that seems interesting or relevant to you.

You should also consider taking an online course to gain more in-depth knowledge and understanding of what you're investigating as a possible passion.

Step 5: Narrow your search.

As you begin reading and researching, you may find one or more career options that jump out at you. Deepen your research on those topics to find out exactly what kind of training or education is needed, who is already successful in this area, what kind of salary you could make, and how long it would take to become proficient in this area.

Start filling in the blanks of all of the details necessary to make this possible passion a reality for you and the structure of your life.

Step 6: Find a mentor.

Find one or two people who are doing what you want to do, and doing it well. Reach out to them. Send them emails to ask if you can get their advice. Make a list of questions you want to ask.

Step 7: Brainstorm and write.

Think about all of the possible action steps you'll need to take to move the needle toward living your passion (once you have done your research). Make one long list of actions, then go back and prioritize and order the list. Break down each action into the smallest possible steps.

Step 8: Take the first action.

Do one concrete thing to get the ball rolling toward your passion. Maybe it's getting your resume in order, signing up for a training class, or making a call to someone. You may not feel 100% sure that this first step is the right step, but you have to take it to find out. So set a date and take it.

If you get stuck, refer back to the previous strategy on setting S.M.A.R.T. quarterly goals. We recommend turning your pursuit of a meaningful career into a project where you take action on a daily basis.

Step 9: Decide on a test drive.

One of the best ways to figure out if a passion *really* is a passion is to test it out. Rather than making a full-on commitment to a new job or starting a business, find a way to get hands-on experience through volunteering, a part-time job, or even shadowing someone for a few days.

This test drive gives you real-world feedback to help you decide if you've truly found what you love.

Step 10: Consider other people.

Remember to keep those close to you involved and in the loop. You will likely meet some resistance. Think ahead about this possibility and how you will handle it. What is the bottom line for you? For them? Keep the lines of communication open.

Step 11: Save money.

Begin putting money aside in a savings account. You may need this as you make your transition to something new. It might be used for additional education or training, to get a business started, or to sustain you financially while you get a business up and running.

Start thinking about ways you can bring in extra cash in a pinch. Even if you transition from one full-time job to another, it's always good to have a back-up plan.

Step 12: Plan your income.

Determine your lowest acceptable yearly income. To do this, you will need to know how you spend your money, where you can (and are willing to) cut back, and how long you are willing to live at this income level. You don't want to go into debt, so this needs to be a realistic number that can sustain a basic lifestyle.

One tool that's great for monitoring your spending and staying on top of your finances is the Mint app. Here, you can enter your billing information, current debt, and bank accounts to get a complete picture of your financial situation. Then you can use Mint to fully understand how much money you need on a monthly basis.

Step 13: Deal with your current job.

Be sure to include as part of your action steps how you will move from your current job into your new one. Will you continue working at your old job as you start your new work? How and when will you discuss this with your employer? Be sure to leave on a good note and handle things professionally so you can maintain those ties.

Step 14: Stay motivated with action.

When moving from something safe and secure to the unknown, it's natural to feel a lot of fear. Thinking, planning, fretting, and pontificating only go so far, and they contribute to your mental clutter.

Daily, focused action will move you forward. If you don't know what to do, just do something. Take one small action in the direction of your dream.

One of the positive outcomes of this 14-step exercise is that you create a sense of purpose as you take control of your life and move toward something more meaningful. In fact, the effort of working toward your passion is sometimes as satisfying as the outcome. Greg Johnson, author of the book *Living Life on Purpose: A Guide to Creating a Life of Success and Significance,* says "Focus on the journey, not the destination. Joy is found not in finishing an activity but in doing it."

Much of our mental distress and negative thinking comes from feeling uncertain and out-of-control about our lives. Once you start taking action toward finding your passion, you'll have more and more mental clarity and peace of mind.

Okay, at this point, you've learned a number of strategies you can use to overcome your negative thought patterns and reduce the impact of life obligations that don't truly matter. In the next section, we'll talk about the negative impact that *some* relationships have on your mental well-being, and what to do about them.

Part III

DECLUTTERING YOUR RELATIONSHIPS

The Negative Impact of Bad Relationships

Your children drive you crazy. Your parents are too needy. Your boss is a jerk. Your spouse doesn't understand you. Your best friend never calls.

How often do you feel irritated, frustrated, or even *furious* with the people in your life?

The answer to this question is important because relationship problems are a leading cause of unhappiness that people feel in life.

We replay unpleasant conversations in our heads and stew for hours over a perceived slight. Or we're detached from our friends and loved ones, only to feel lonely, isolated, and unloved.

We create false mental narratives about other people, assigning to them thoughts and behaviors that may or may not be true, but that feel hurtful and overwhelming nonetheless.

Now, it's true that you can't coexist with others without the occasional misunderstanding. However, if you find that most interactions leave you emotionally drained, then you should look for ways to either improve these relationships or remove certain people from your life.

Imagine if you had no anxiety related to the people in your life. How much less cluttered would your mind be? How much more energy could you put toward productive, positive pursuits?

Although the important people in our lives can be the source of mental distress, our close relationships remain one of the fundamental components in life contributing to long-term happiness.

Can Great Relationships Lead to Happiness?

One of the longest studies ever conducted on happiness is the Harvard Study of Adult Development, previously known as the Grant Study in Social Adjustments. Since 1937, researchers at Harvard have been examining the question of what makes us happy by following 268 men who entered college in the late 1930s. They have followed them through war, career, marriage and divorce, parenthood and grandparenthood, and old age.

Robert Waldinger, the psychiatrist and Harvard Medical School professor who currently leads the study, says the long-term research is unequivocal: "Close relationships and social connections keep you happy and healthy. That is the bottom line. People who were more concerned with achievement or less concerned with connection were less happy. Basically, humans are wired for personal connections."

How is it that relationships can contribute so much to our happiness while also being a huge source of our mental fatigue? The key is not just having relationships—it's having *high-quality* relationships. Whether with a romantic partner, friend, family member, or even work associate, a high-quality relationship involves:

- Prioritizing the relationship
- Open communication
- Healthy conflict resolution
- Mutual trust and respect
- Shared interests
- Some level of emotional and/or intellectual intimacy
- Acceptance and forgiveness
- Physical touch (for personal relationships)

It's in our best interest to be proactive about how we choose the people in our lives and how we choose to interact with them. Creating, maintaining, and nurturing good relationships is necessary for our well-being and peace of mind.

Rather than looking to others to make relationship changes, the **best place to start is within you**. Even if your family members, friends, and business associates need to improve their relationship skills, you can go a long way in reducing stress in your life by initiating changes in you. You can't change others, anyway—you only have the power to control how *you* interact with and react to the people around you.

Let's look at four ways you can improve your relationships, which can have a direct, positive impact on your mindset.

Relationship Strategy #1: Be More Present

A University of North Carolina study of "relatively happy, nondistressed couples" revealed that couples who actively practiced mindfulness saw improvements to their relationship happiness. They also enjoyed healthier levels of "relationship stress, stress coping efficacy, and overall stress." The practice of mindfulness allows us to be present with our partners, to be less emotionally reactive with them, and to more quickly overcome stressful situations in the relationship.

Relationship presence doesn't just apply to romantic couples. You can practice mindfulness in all of your relationships.

What does it mean to be more present in your relationships?

Here are a few strategies you can practice:

Practice Empathic Listening

Have you ever noticed that some people don't listen closely during a conversation?

For many folks, it's hard to pay attention because our minds are full of so many thoughts. Often, when someone is talking, our mind is more focused on the minutia of our lives, our worries, or what we want to say next.

Empathic (or active) listening is a willingness to step outside of your distracted mind and listen to their words in a non-judgmental way. Empathy is the grace note of empathic listening, as it allows the speaker to feel safe, validated, and understood.

Active listening isn't part of a conversation in the traditional sense. There's no give and take, sharing dialogue, or competing to talk. With empathic listening, it's all about the other person and what they are trying to communicate—with their words, with the words left unspoken, and with their emotions.

As an empathic listener, you must be willing to:

- Allow the other person to dominate the conversation and determine the topic discussed.
- Remain completely attentive to what the other person is saying.
- Avoid interrupting, even when you have something important to add.
- Ask open-ended questions that invite more from the speaker.
- Avoid coming to premature conclusions or offering solutions.
- Reflect back to the speaker what you heard them say.

It may seem that empathic listening only provides benefits for the speaker, but as the listener you are in a state of focused awareness. When you listen empathically, it's impossible to be stuck in looping thoughts or distracted by worry or regret.

You can start practicing empathic listening with your partner, family members, and close friends. In your next interaction, commit to 10 minutes of active listening where you are focused solely on the other person and what they are saying. This will bring you closer to your loved one and also give you a break from your cluttered thoughts.

Mindful Speaking

Negative thinking can have a damaging impact on the quality of your relationships. If your language is filled with fearful comments, self-condemnation, disparaging remarks about others, or self-pity, you do nothing more than convince others that you are a negative person to be around.

On other hand, when you focus on fostering positive interactions, you can strengthen the relationships you do have. For instance, Dr. John Gottman discovered through his research that there should be **five times as many positive interactions between partners as there are negative in order for a relationship to be stable and a marriage to last.** Gottman's findings can be applied to other relationships as well. Conflict and negativity tend to push people away.

Awareness is always the first step toward change. We recommend paying close attention to what you say during a conversation, particularly in your love relationship. Place a mental filter between your thoughts and words, recognizing the power your words have on one of the most important people in your life.

Resist the temptation to simply react to someone's words or actions. Take a moment to choose your words carefully. Speak in ways that are loving, compassionate, and respectful, and try to use a calm, non-threatening voice, even if the other person is agitated or angry.

As you speak more mindfully, those around you will often respond in kind. Even if they don't, you empower yourself to maintain self-control and inner peace.

Through the practice of mindful speaking, you not only improve the quality of your relationships, but also improve the quality of your inner world.

Loving Kindness Meditation

A loving kindness meditation focuses on developing feelings of warmth towards others. You can use a loving kindness meditation specifically to improve your relationships with specific people in your life in order to reduce negative thinking about them.

This kind of meditation cultivates our awareness of others as human beings deserving of compassion and love—even when they are being difficult—which can decrease relationship conflicts and improve your own well-being. There are three studies that support this claim.

First, scientists from Stanford University found that meditation that focuses on loving kindness increases people's feelings of social connectedness.

Also, according to a University of Utah study, loving kindness meditation practice "decreased overall levels of perceived hostility, insensitivity, interference, and ridicule from others." This special meditation practice will not only improve your intimate relationships, but your relationship with you as well.

Finally, in a landmark study, researchers found that practicing seven weeks of loving kindness meditation increased feelings of love, joy, contentment, gratitude, pride, hope, interest, amusement, and awe.

You can practice a loving kindness meditation anywhere, but start with a short 10-minute meditation in a quiet place without distraction.

Here is a simple process for practicing this habit:

- Sit in a comfortable position, either on the floor with your legs crossed and your hands sitting loosely in your lap, or sitting up straight in a chair with your legs uncrossed, feet on the floor, and hands resting in your lap.

- Close your eyes and take two or three deep cleansing breathes, and then begin counting each breath, going from 1 to 10.

- One you are relaxed, bring to mind a person to whom you wish to send loving kindness, and consider their positive qualities—the light of goodness you see in them.

- After you focus on their positive qualities for a few minutes, mentally say the following statements directed to your loved one: "May you be happy," "May you be well," "May you be loved."

  There is nothing wrong with altering the words slightly to focus on the needs of the individual. There are no hard and fast rules. You might substitute the person's name rather than saying "you."

  You could also add thoughts like:

  May you be free from inner and outer harm and danger.

  May you be safe and protected.

  May you be free of mental suffering or distress.

  May you be free of physical pain and suffering.

  May you be healthy and strong.

  May you be able to live in this world happily, peacefully, joyfully, with ease.

Not only will this meditation practice improve your relationships, but it also will increase your emotional well-being and peace of mind. How you adapt the practice to your personal circumstances is ultimately up to ~~but it remains at its heart a deeply transformative process in your~~

"Let us not look at the talents we wish we had or pine away for the gifts that are not ours, but instead do the best we can with what we have." – B.J. Richardson

Comparing ourselves unfavorably to other people is one of the major causes of mental turmoil and emotional suffering.

- "If only I were as attractive as my friend."
- "Why can't I be as smart as my brother?"
- "They have so much more money than we do."
- "She travels all the time, and I never get to go anywhere."

These thoughts can spiral out of control, making us feel bad about ourselves while viewing *other people* as the cause of our unhappiness. By measuring ourselves against the achievements, possessions, or traits of everyone else, we set the stage for the disintegration of potentially fulfilling relationships.

In their work as authors and entrepreneurs, Steve and Barrie have seen how easy it is to make comparisons with those who have achieved more success. "I have fallen into the trap of measuring myself against my peers," says Barrie. "It undermines my focus on the work I'm doing, making me feel inept and envious until I regain my footing and realize I'm on my own journey, which *should* be different from those around me."

Comparison fosters so many negative feelings that it destroys more than just your peace of mind—it damages your relationships. The more you ruminate about how you measure up, the worse you feel about both you and the other person. Feelings of envy, jealously, shame, guilt, embarrassment, self-loathing, resentment, and anger are not qualities that enhance a relationship or make you attractive to others.

Gretchen Rubin, author of the New York Times #1 bestselling book *The Happiness Project*, says "Negative emotions like loneliness, envy, and guilt have an important role to play in a happy life; they're big, flashing signs that something needs to change."

We all compare ourselves from time to time, and sometimes comparing can motivate us to improve ourselves or to achieve something that we observe in others. But when comparison causes those "big, flashing signs" to light up, it's time to take action.

It does take mental effort to disengage from comparing and the emotions that go along with it. But changing your reactions to those who have "more" will free you up to follow your own path and become the best person YOU are meant to be.

Here are **three simple and short practices** that can help you end the practice of comparing yourself to others:

Practice #1: Practice radical self-acceptance.

No amount of comparing, fretting, and ruminating will change who you are, how you look, what you've achieved, or what you own in this moment. The person you are right now is all you've got, at least for today.

Rather than resisting this person, lean into it. Accept it, and acknowledge that you are perfectly okay right now. Simply adopting this moment of radical self-acceptance is liberating and empowering.

Practice #2: Change what you can.

American theologian Reinhold Niebuhr is known for writing *The Serenity Prayer*, in which he states:

God grant me the serenity

To accept the things I cannot change;

The courage to change the things I can;

And the wisdom to know the difference

with realism.

Comparing yourself to others you admire can inspire you to change for the better, to step up your game, and to improve your life. But sometimes, no matter how hard you may try, you will never be able to match the accomplishments of a particular person. You may never look like your fashion model friend or become as wealthy as your millionaire cousin.

Rather than blindly longing for something you don't have, make decisions through the filter of your inner wisdom. What *can* you change? What do you *want* to change? Go back to your values and life priorities to help you define your life on your own terms rather than trying to emulate someone else who may have differing values and priorities.

You may still occasionally long for something you can't have, but do the best you can with what you do have. Focus on your strengths and continue to practice self-acceptance.

Practice #3: Express gratitude constantly.

Comparisons blind us to all that we already have. We become so focused on what someone else has and how we don't measure up that we neglect to acknowledge all of the blessings around us.

It's a matter of choosing to see the glass half full rather than half empty—and acknowledging your gratitude for the water in the glass.

When you wake up in the morning, before you get out of bed, make a mental list of everything good in your life and focus on each blessing for a minute or two. Do this before you go to sleep as well.

You can reinforce feelings of gratitude by writing them in a gratitude journal. At the end of the day, mentally review everything positive that occurred and write it down. Take a moment to consider what your life would be like without the people you love, your home, your health, etc. When you consider having your blessings taken away from you, it becomes very clear how blessed you are.

Relationship Strategy #2: Getting

We talked earlier in the book about ruminating on the past, and how it can cause those feelings of being mentally overwhelmed. When you think about the past, you may notice that many of your thoughts relate to encounters with the current people in your life.

You replay conversations that were unpleasant or hurtful. You dwell on a broken relationship or a lost love. Maybe you reflect with longing and sadness about children who have grown and moved out of the house, friends who have drifted away, or siblings who seem disconnected.

Perhaps you encountered relationship pain that was so deep and wounding you have never really healed from it, and it continues to disrupt your life and sabotage your thoughts. Looping these memories can trigger unresolved anger, shame, guilt, fear, and sadness.

Because relationships are so integral to our lives, it's not surprising that people from our pasts continue to cause us pain weeks, months, or even *years* after an encounter or relationship has ended. You replay these "mind movies" so often that you start to identify with them. Dragging the past around in this way is a heavy burden that drains you of energy and inner peace.

Sometimes we replay past situations in an unconscious attempt to resolve them, but ruminating only keeps us stuck in the past and miserable in the present. How can we break free from our thoughts about the past so they don't continue to imprison us or bind us to people who should no longer be part of our lives?

Eckhart Tolle, author of *The Power of Now, says* "We can learn to break the habit of accumulating and perpetuating old emotion by flapping our wings, metaphorically speaking, and refrain from mentally dwelling on the past, regardless of whether something happened yesterday or 30 years ago. We can learn not to keep situations or events alive in our minds, but to return our attention continuously to the pristine, timeless present moment rather than be caught up in mental movie making."

Easier said than done, right?

It's hard to just drop painful memories and push these thoughts out of our minds.

Hard...*but not impossible.*

And certainly worth the effort if you want to free yourself to enjoy positive, loving relationships in your current life.

If you want to be present with your family and friends today, you can't remain stuck in your thoughts about past relationships and old hurts.

Here are some ways you can clear the clutter of negative thoughts about the past:

Resolve what you can.

If there's an unresolved problem or hurt between you and another person, **take action to resolve the situation**. Rather than stewing about the past issue, initiate communication with the other person to talk through it, even if you feel you were "wronged." It's hard to reach out to someone who has hurt you, but the discomfort of doing this is far less than the slow torment of lingering on past pain.

Feelings of anger or hurt can make open dialog difficult, but learn more about healthy communication so you can have a productive talk with the other person.

Part of resolution might include sharing your feelings and pain, listening to the other person's perspective, offering or asking for forgiveness, and discussing the future of the relationship. Break the "spell" of your internal story about the past by talking about it openly.

Having a productive conversation with someone from your past isn't always possible, but when it is, it can be the best way to release you from feeling trapped by your memories and pain.

Challenge your story.

situation from any other angle.

You may believe your memories and interpretation of the relationship are correct, but the other person may have an entirely different perspective.

Challenge your own interpretation by stepping into the other person's shoes. You can do this by answering these questions:

- How might they see what happened between you?
- What could you have said or done that they might have misinterpreted?
- Is it possible that your memories are incorrect?
- Does the other person have a valid point of view?
- Is it possible that things didn't occur exactly as you believe they did?

When you empathize with the other person, it removes some of the pain or anger associated with the memory. By challenging your own beliefs and memories, you give yourself permission to view the situation from a less negative point of view.

Offer forgiveness.

The person from your past may never apologize, but offer forgiveness anyway. You don't have to forgive them in person, but forgive them inside your own heart and mind.

Clinging to your anger and pain only prolongs suffering and mental distress. You forgive to set *yourself* free from this suffering so you can move on to live in the present with a clear mind.

Bestselling self-improvement author Dr. Wayne Dyer says, "Forgiving others is essential for spiritual growth. Your experience of someone who has hurt you, while painful, is now nothing more than a thought or feeling that you carry around. These thoughts of resentment, anger, and hatred represent slow, debilitating energies that will dis empower you if you continue to let these thoughts occupy space in your head. If you could release them, you would know more peace."

Forgiving someone doesn't necessarily mean you reconcile with them. It means you let go of resentment and anger so it doesn't further poison you. It may be hard to forgive, especially when the offending person hasn't accepted responsibility for their behavior. But you can begin by recognizing this person is doing the best they know how with the skills they possess. When you find yourself ruminating about their past offenses, shift your thoughts away from them and to yourself. Acknowledge your feelings without blaming the other person for them. Ask yourself, "What have I learned from this? How can I use it to improve myself?"

As Dr. Dyer says, "Your life is like a play with several acts. Some of the characters who enter have short roles to play, others, much larger. Some are villains and others are good guys. But all of them are necessary, otherwise they wouldn't be in the play. Embrace them all, and move on to the next act."

Offering forgiveness might require you forgive yourself for something you said or did in a relationship. Reflect honestly on your actions and how they might have hurt or offended the other person. You'll likely come up with many reasons why you behaved as you did, and perhaps have some legitimate rationalizations for your actions. But if there is any part of your behavior that was wrong, you must accept it and forgive yourself for it.

It becomes easier to forgive yourself when you shift your perspective about past mistakes. Rather than beating yourself up over past relationship mistakes, try to honor the past and see your actions as a blessing. They were part of who you were at the time, and you needed to learn from them. Now you can move on and forgive yourself, knowing who you want to be and how you want to behave.

The two previous strategies we've discussed apply to any relationship in your life. But your intimate love relationship stands apart as one that deserves special attention.

With your spouse or romantic partner, you have the opportunity for tremendous emotional and personal growth, especially if you view your partner as someone who is in your life to teach you something. It's through this relationship that you can learn to be more present and compassionate.

Ironically, our love relationships tend to present us with the biggest challenges in our lives, causing the most "mental clutter" and distress. Practicing mindfulness in your love relationship gives you a tool for strengthening your intimate connection while reducing stress and angst in your life.

Mindfulness expert and Professor of Medicine Emeritus Jon Kabat-Zinn describes mindfulness as paying attention to the present moment with intention, while letting go of judgment.

This practice might seem impossible in the heat of an argument when you just want to lash out at your partner. But with practice, mindfulness increases our awareness of what we are experiencing with our partners, and allows us the space to determine how we want to act (and react) with them.

When you're able to bypass emotional reactions with your spouse or partner, you feel more centered, calm, and capable of resolving issues in a loving manner. This ability alone can save you from days and even years of mental and emotional distress that depletes your emotional energy.

"Mindfulness isn't about denying or burying our emotions," says psychologist and author Dr. Lisa Firestone in an article for *Psychology Today*. "It's simply about cultivating a different relationship to our feelings and experiences, in which we are in the driver's seat. We can see our feelings and thoughts like a passing train roaring through the station, but we alone choose if we want to get on board."

Choosing not to get on board is the beginning of a conscious relationship that promotes healing and intimacy rather than discord and divisiveness. Here are some simple actions you can take to become more present in your marriage or love relationship:

Make the commitment.

With the awareness that mindfulness will improve the quality of your connection with your partner, commit yourself to practicing this habit on a daily basis.

If you've spent years in an unconscious relationship in which you and your partner are reactive, it will take some time to retrain yourself to interact differently. But if you're motivated to grow in your relationship and reduce stress in your life, you can change.

This is the most important relationship in your life, and it impacts your mental health and your outlook on everything. Commit to this one practice in your relationship, and you'll see an improvement in all areas of your life.

Put a note in a place you will see it first thing in the morning to remind you to be present with your spouse when you interact. You may need reminders in several places in the house when you begin this practice.

Communicate your commitment.

Your decision to be more mindful with your partner isn't predicated by your partner's mutual commitment—but it certainly helps.

Sit down with your spouse when you can talk without interruption and let him or her know about your new plan. You might say something like, "I've decided I want to be more present and compassionate in my relationship with you. It will make us closer and will help us resolve our differences without as much anger or hurt. I've made a commitment to this, and I'd like it if you'd commit to it as well."

Your spouse may wonder exactly what this means, and this leads to the

Be emotionally present.

Being emotionally present means being fully attuned to your partner in conversation. If your partner is in pain, it means remaining emotionally open to the pain, and showing empathy.

It also means paying attention to your partner's body language and reflecting it back, as well as using eye contact, gentle touch, and nodding to show you hear your partner.

It generally doesn't mean offering suggestions or ways to "fix" a situation unless your partner asks for that. In fact, we block our innate ability for emotional presence when we try to do something "more" for our partner. Attuned presence allows your partner to feel less alone with his or her feelings.

This kind of emotional resonance with your spouse leads to more intimacy, trust, and security in your relationship.

Listen without defensiveness.

When you and your partner have a conflict or emotionally charged conversation, presence means you listen without preparing your response or defense.

Be aware of your own reactive emotions, name them, and recognize that they have been triggered, but don't act on them. Try to pull your attention back to your partner's words, and acknowledge that your partner's feelings are as important as your own.

Reflect back to your partner.

The willingness to reflect back to your partner the words you hear from them shows that you are actively listening. It also reinforces for your spouse that you care enough to seek to fully understand what that are saying to you.

Reflecting back isn't simply parroting what your partner says. It's a way of confirming that what you heard is actually what your partner meant. It opens dialog for clarification and invites discussion about mutual resolution and understanding.

This is a highly valuable mindfulness technique during times of conflict, hurt feelings, or misunderstandings.

Communicate authentically.

Being present with your partner is a mature relationship skill. It means you can't respond or react in childlike ways, using passive-aggressive words or behaviors like eye rolling, the silent treatment, or sulking. Throwing tantrums or having angry outbursts <u>always</u> prevents open, authentic communication.

When you have an issue with your spouse, rather than taking a jab at them or making a disparaging comment, turn back to the practice of mindfulness. Pay attention to your emotions and wait until you are calm and less defensive before initiating a conversation.

Share the issue without blame or criticism. State your perception of the issue, how it made you feel, and what you need from your partner in order to restore your connection. Listen to your partner's response and perspective without defensiveness.

Look for lessons within conflict.

We mentioned earlier that your love relationship is the laboratory for personal growth if you pay attention. Conflict is uncomfortable and unpleasant, but it provides the perfect opportunity for learning.

Rather than stewing in your angry juices after a conflict, ask yourself these questions:

- Is it possible that I'm not entirely right?
- Is my partner's perspective valid to some extent?
- Am I being the person I want to be with my partner?

- What have I learned from this conflict?

- How do I want to change as a result of this interaction?

Your answers to these questions will foster healing and self-awareness, and allow you to break free from the inner critic who keeps you agitated and angry.

Spend quality time with your partner without distraction.

One of the most valuable things you can do for the health of your relationship is to spend quality time with your partner. This is time when you are both relaxed and engaged without the pressures of work, children, or conflict.

Busy couples often have to schedule this time because life is so hectic and demanding. If that's the case for you, make a point to arrange a regular date or even 30 minutes of daily quiet time with your spouse where you can talk and reconnect.

The more emotional intimacy you share with your partner, the more you insulate your relationship from the conflicts that create suffering for you both. Putting in this effort is an investment in your peace of mind and mental clarity.

Relationship Strategy #4: Let Go of Certain People

Decluttering your relationships sometimes means just that—letting go of people who cause you suffering. Sometimes the only course of action is to say goodbye to those who continue to undermine your mental and emotional health.

Letting go of a relationship is painful, even if it's draining you, holding you back, blinding you to your true self, or, worse yet, toxic or abusive.

We invest a lot in our friendships, our marriages, our business partners, and our family members.

Quite often, it's one of these close relationships—a person or people with whom we've been intimately and deeply involved for many years—that cause us the most pain and turmoil.

At some point in one of these relationships, you will reach the point where the pain and difficulty outweigh the positives—where the fallout of letting go seems less daunting than the misery of staying put.

For instance, one of the hardest things Steve ever had to do was to cut off all communication with an ex-girlfriend. After an extremely frustrating yearlong relationship, he felt that there was no way he could have her in his life—even as a friend. Their interaction was just too toxic for both people to find any happiness around one another.

So he made the decision to "force" a permanent separation by going to Europe and spending eight months traveling without any access to a cell phone. While it was challenging, Steve knew that the only way to move on was to create a "cold turkey" situation where it would be almost impossible for the two of them to have any sort of conversation.

Now, you don't have leave your country in order to escape from a bad relationship, but you might want to consider taking a proactive approach to eliminate certain people from your life—and make sure you stick to this plan.

- Verbal, emotional, or physical abuse
- Consistent dishonesty, disloyalty, or deceit
- Divergent core values or questionable integrity
- General toxicity, negativity, and incompatibility
- Consistent, harmful irresponsibility
- Ongoing immaturity and emotional manipulation
- Unresolved or untreated mental health issues
- Addictions (drugs, alcohol, sex, gambling, pornography)
- Refusal to communicate, address problems, or invest in the relationship

Beyond these more serious situations, sometimes a relationship simply runs its course. You may find, for reasons you don't completely understand, that another person diminishes your life more than enlivens it. You may come to a point where you simply don't wish to deal with the emotional clutter and chaos another person creates in your life.

If the person causing your suffering happens to be your spouse, a parent or family member, or an adult child, you can't just abandon the relationship without serious repercussions. But you can better manage these relationships and protect your mental health by creating strong boundaries and communicating your boundaries to the person involved. You can learn more about creating relationship boundaries in this post (http://bit.ly/2aHqsZ0) on Barrie's blog, *Live Bold and Bloom*.

If you have difficult parents and extended family members who are causing you angst, you can learn how to deal with them in this article (http://bit.ly/2aZZH4s); or, if your marriage is unhappy and you're considering divorce, you might want to check out this post (http://bit.ly/2aHqQXx).

Of course, managing or letting go of any relationship is not a quick proposition. It can take months or years and a lot of heartache to detach from someone who has been a part of your life in any significant way.

But we would be remiss if we didn't include this point as part of your mental declutter options.

Here are some thoughts on how to remove yourself from a draining or painful relationship:

Consider the positives of life without this person.

Letting go of a relationship might feel like you're giving up or being unkind. You might feel guilty if you step away from this person. But if the relationship is causing you regular discomfort, you are not treating *yourself* with respect.

If you're having trouble deciding whether or not to end (or contain) the relationship, think about how your life would feel if you didn't have this person around you. Would you feel relieved? Liberated? Less anxious or stressed?

Ask yourself how your life might change for the better if you didn't have to cope with the problems and concerns associated with your interactions with this person. Your judgment might be clouded by your feelings of guilt or obligation, but try to honestly weigh the positives of letting go.

Consider the fallout of saying goodbye.

Ending a relationship rarely occurs without some fallout. Your decision will likely impact other people close to you, forcing them to choose sides or at least take some kind of stand—which might not be in your favor. Some people might cut you off as a result.

The person you are saying goodbye to may try to sabotage you, talk behind your back, or wound you in some way. Their reaction may be more dramatic or damaging than you anticipated, causing things to get worse before they get better. You might find the loss of the relationship more painful than you thought it would be, and you second-guess yourself.

It's valuable to think through all of the possible repercussions before you end the relationship. How will each of these scenarios make your

Define what "goodbye" really means.

Letting go might mean a permanent end to a relationship where there is no communication or interaction at all. But this isn't possible or reasonable for all relationships. Goodbye might also mean letting go of the old way of relating to this person and implementing a new, more self-protective way.

Relationships you have with family members, adult children, or a former spouse can't always be cut off entirely. But you can create boundaries around the time spent with these people and how you communicate with them in order to protect your mental and emotional health.

Decide what "goodbye" means for you exactly. How much time are you willing to spend with this person? How do you wish to communicate with them, and how often? What will you no longer tolerate in your interactions with them? Being proactive about these decisions makes you feel more in control and calm about how to move forward.

Communicate your intentions without blame.

Simply dropping a friend or family member cold turkey, with no explanation or conversation, might be the easy way out—but it isn't the kindest way. Yes, this person might be draining every last drop of energy and joy out of you, but they are still deserving of an explanation, or at least a head's up.

You don't need to get into a long, drawn-out conflict in order to say goodbye or cut back on your interactions. Nor do you need to assign blame or cast aspersions. Try to take the high road and say what *you* would want to hear if the shoe were on the other foot.

Person-to-person conversations are generally the best way to have this talk, but you know this person best. If you anticipate a lot of drama or anger, then maybe a letter or phone call is better than meeting in person.

Either way, try to keep it short and focus on *your own feelings* rather than *their faults.*

You might say something like, "I need a break from our friendship because I feel like we are out of sync, and it's causing me distress. I care about you, but I need to step away. I didn't want to back off without saying something first."

Create a plan for a negative reaction.

No matter how kindly you end a relationship, the other person (and perhaps others you are both associated with) will react badly. It's hard to anticipate how someone might react when they are hurt or angry.

Try to prepare for this potential fallout in advance. This might mean you ask a support person to be with you when you communicate your intentions, as well as after the difficult conversation.

You might need to talk personally about your plan to end this relationship with friends and family who know the other person. Try to explain your need to end the relationship without bad-mouthing the other person if possible.

Depending on the intensity and longevity of the relationship you are ending, you might need the help of a therapist so you can navigate your own feelings of loss and pain.

Accept that it can be a process.

For some relationships, letting go is a slow backing away over time. Or it might be an ending followed by a period of reconciliation, only to result in a more permanent ending.

Sometimes guilt, confusion, or loneliness can make you second-guess your decision to let go. It takes going back to the relationship to cement your determination to finally end it.

Recognize that letting go of someone who was once close to you is rarely easy or pain-free. Give yourself permission to do it slowly if that's the best way for you.

Allow yourself to grieve.

The ending of a relationship that was on
someday work out is painful. Yes, you may feel relief that you don't have
to deal with the difficult aspects of the relationship. You may have more
emotional energy and fewer daily frustrations. However, grief has a way
of sneaking up on us when we least expect it. Any process of letting go
can create a pocket of grief that needs time to heal.

Don't try to talk yourself out of your grief or second-guess your decision
because your grief is confusing. If you view grief as a normal part of the
process of letting go, it will pass through you more quickly, allowing
you to regain the peace of mind and joy that was diminished during the
relationship.

As you can see, eliminating people from your life can be challenging,
but also rewarding because it frees you up to spend time with the people
who truly matter.

In the next section, we'll go over the fourth area that you can declutter
in order to reduce stress, anxiety, and a feeling overwhelming your life.

Let's get to it....

Part IV

DECLUTTERING YOUR SURROUNDINGS

The Value of Decluttering Your Surroundings

"If people concentrated on the really important things in life, there'd be a shortage of fishing poles."

– Doug Larson

Where you choose to spend time every day ultimately determines the quality of your life. We know that's an obvious statement, but many people fail to analyze what they do on a moment-to-moment, day-by-day basis.

In fact, we tend to allow happenstance, boredom, or other people to determine how we spend a lot of our time. We *react* to what's in front of us, instead of *mindfully deciding* how we want to *create* our lives.

We talked earlier about defining your values, life priorities, goals, and life passion. These actions help you direct the daily activities of your life. But you can't focus on these big-picture actions all day, every day. That's because the bulk of your time is often filled with mindless tasks that contribute to feelings of overwhelm, emptiness, and mental clutter.

We've become attached to things, routines, and environments. We allow our homes to become repositories for every new whim as we accumulate more and more stuff over the years. We're obsessed with technology and spend hours on social media, taking and sharing "selfies," and documenting the minutiae of our lives.

So to get the full benefit of mental decluttering your life, you need to address the more mundane but potentially depleting aspects of daily life. These mindless activities are the small holes in the dam that allow your energy and joy to seep out. With a few changes, you can plug the holes and refill your tank.

In this section, we'll tackle the final step of the process—how to declutter your immediate surroundings in order to free up mental space for the important goals and people in your life.

Simplify Your Home

"Have nothing in your house that you do not know to be useful, or believe to be beautiful."

– William Morris

Your home should be a haven—a place where you feel peaceful, happy, and calm. But can you feel this way when your home is cluttered with stuff?

Researchers at the Princeton University Neuroscience Institute published the results of a study they conducted in *The Journal of Neuroscience* that relates directly to uncluttered and organized living. According to their report, "Interactions of Top-Down and Bottom-Up Mechanisms in Human Visual Cortex":

> *Multiple stimuli present in the visual field at the same time compete for neural representation by mutually suppressing their evoked activity throughout visual cortex, providing a neural correlate for the limited processing capacity of the visual system.*

In other word, when your environment is cluttered, the visual chaos restricts your ability to focus. The clutter also limits your brain's ability to process information. Clutter distracts you so you're unable to process information as well as you would in an uncluttered, organized, and serene environment.

For a moment, visualize a room with minimal furniture, free of clutter and extraneous knick-knacks. The room is tidy, organized, and minimal.

See yourself sitting in this room and notice how you feel.

Now visualize a room packed with furniture, magazines and books stacked on the tables, and every surface adorned with clutter and stuff.

How do you feel sitting in this room?

Clutter steals your focus, making you feel overwhelmed, distracted, and agitated. Your brain is so busy trying to process all of the visual stimuli that you can't fully enjoy the moment.

Now maybe you feel sentimental about many of the objects in your home. But we invite you to embrace a new mindset about physical clutter and how it impacts your mental health. Decluttering your home might be a process that takes several iterations before you feel comfortable saying goodbye to things. But by simply starting the process, you'll be surprised at the positive impact it has on your energy and state of mind.

Steve and Barrie have written about how to declutter your home in their book *10-Minute Declutter: The Stress Free Habit for Simplifying Your Home,* where you'll find detailed ideas on decluttering and organizing every room in your house.

You can declutter your home in less time than you think—and without feeling completely overwhelmed—when you tackle it in small chunks of time every day. Set aside just 10 minutes a day to work on your clutter, and within a few weeks your house will be in order.

Here is a 10-step process from the book to help you get started:

1. Set up a staging area.

You'll need a place to temporarily stage all of the items you want to store elsewhere or give away. Find a room or space in your house where you can place these things until you're ready to deal with them. You may decide to create a staging area in each room you're working on rather than one main area. This works just fine as well, as long as you don't mind having a pile of stuff sitting in a corner of the room.

2. Get boxes for the staging area.

You'll need boxes in varying sizes for staging items to donate, give to other people, sell, or put into storage. Use inexpensive cardboard boxes for staging purposes. Later, you can purchase more durable storage containers for any items you want to store.

3. Have a timer, notebook, and pen handy.

Since you'll be working in 10-minute increments, set a timer so you'll know when to stop. You'll be surprised at how much you can accomplish in 10 minutes. Also, keep a notebook and pen with you as you declutter and organize.

You'll want to make notes on organizing supplies you may need to purchase or ideas you have for storage, donation, or selling items.

4. Set up a schedule.

Setting up a 10-minute declutter schedule means you're adding a new habit to your day, which can be hard. Creating habits requires a few special skills to make sure you don't give up. Choose the time of day you want to perform your declutter habit. Make sure it immediately follows a previously established habit like having your coffee in the morning or brushing your teeth. This trigger will cue you to perform your declutter habit. Then reward yourself after you perform your new habit.

For more on this, check out Steve's article on how to build a habit in eight steps (http://bit.ly/2aBWv0K).

5. Begin where you spend most of your time.

If you're confused about where to start your decluttering and organizing project, we suggest you begin where you spend the most time. For most people, that would be the kitchen, bedrooms, and family room. When you complete a room you use a lot, you'll get a great feeling of satisfaction, as well as a boost of emotional energy and peace of mind.

6. Determine your system.

In order to keep your work to 10 minutes a day, consider moving through spaces top to bottom, left to right. For example, in your kitchen, begin with the top shelves of cabinets and declutter/clean the shelves on the left side first, then move to the right.

Remove everything from the left side shelves, then quickly sort what you know you want to put back onto the shelves. Wipe the shelf clean, and then replace the items you want to keep. Put the remaining items in the appropriate boxes to give away, sell, donate, or store elsewhere. With drawers, do the same—dump everything out, sort the absolute keepers, wipe out the drawer, replace the keepers, and put the rest in the appropriate boxes.

7. Avoid indecision.

One reason people have a hard time decluttering is because they can't decide whether or not to let something go. There are a million and one reasons for this confusion, but you need to deal with indecision in the moment to successfully declutter.

That's why we suggest you put only the absolute keepers back in the spaces you've decluttered. Get rid of anything you know for sure you don't want or need. Anything you feel slightly ambivalent about or rarely use, put into a storage box to deal with later. Label the box, seal it up, and put it into a storage room.

8. Work quickly.

Have you noticed how easy it's to get distracted when you're cleaning and organizing? You pick something up, look at it, think about it, wonder what to do with it. With the 10-minute system, you've created a sense of urgency for yourself.

You're trying to accomplish a task in a short amount of time. That's why it's so important to replace only the items you know you need. You can deal with the other questionable items later. You may discover you don't need them at all after living without them in sight for a while.

9. Tell your family.

Be sure you inform those who live in the house with you that you are working on this declutter project. Better yet, ask for their support and help to complete the project even more quickly. At the very least, you want to be sure they don't come behind you and re-clutter the spaces you've completed. If you have kids, it's great to get them involved in 10-minute cleanup projects. They'll enjoy racing against the clock to complete a task.

10. Enjoy the process.

Even the smallest accomplishments afford a great sense of satisfaction and pride. Every day, you'll complete a small task that will lead to a streamlined, organized, tidy home. But rather than seeing these daily tasks as simply a means to that end, try to enjoy each 10-minute chunk of time. Put on some music and make it fun. Give yourself a nice reward once you complete the task—a cup of tea, reading for a few minutes, or a walk outside.

Marie Kondo, author of the book *The Life-Changing Magic of Tidying Up*, says "The space in which we live should be for the person we are becoming now, not for the person we were in the past."

If you have a strong attachment to the past, whether through your thinking or your clutter, you cause yourself suffering. Let go. Release the physical objects that weigh you down. Focus your mind and your daily life on the present, and you'll feel liberated and unencumbered.

Simplify Your Digital Life

There's a lot of good that's come from the explosion of technology and digital communication. It has definitely made our lives easier, faster, and more productive. But there is a diminishing point of return with our devotion to digital devices.

We've become obsessed with technology, and it's impacting every aspect of how we live our lives. We are slaves to the gadgets that were supposed to simplify our lives, and prefer the quick fix of instant information and low-quality entertainment over real-world interactions and experiences.

We spend hours on social media. Our inboxes are flooded. Our desktops are littered. Our laptops are bursting at the seams with more documents, photos, and downloads than we can absorb in a lifetime.

Digital "stuff" has an insidious way of occupying your time with non-essential activities—and just like physical clutter in your home, digital clutter creates feelings of anxiety, agitation, and overwhelm.

In the book *10-Minute Digital Declutter: The Simple Habit to Eliminate Technology Overload*, Barrie and Steve remind:

> *If you add up the time spent on each digital device, every day, then you probably have a closer relationship with the virtual world than you have with your spouse, children, or friends. You know there's something wrong with this balance, and yet you still find yourself flipping open the lid or gazing at your iPhone whenever you have a moment to spare—or even when you don't. Is this really how you want to live your life?*

From this book, we recommend a few actions to consider to support your mental declutter habits.

How are you spending your digital time?

Take a realistic look at how you spend your time on your devices. Of course there are necessary online activities for your personal and professional life. But then there are the hours you spend plugged in just surfing the net, playing games, and checking in on social media.

Spend a few minutes reviewing your day and add up the non-essential time you spent plugged in. Better yet, document your digital activities throughout the day. You'll be surprised at how much time you give away to virtual experiences.

All of this digital input creates agitation and has an addictive quality that pulls you away from more meaningful pursuits that energize you rather than depleting you.

Where and how can you begin cutting back?

Start with an hour a day that you hold sacred and free from any digital time. Shut down your computer and put your phone into a drawer. What can you do instead of engaging in digital distractions?

We suggest you...

- Read a book
- Talk a long walk
- Exercise
- Talk with a friend
- Spend quality time with your spouse and children
- Do something creative, like writing or drawing
- Learn a new skill
- Meditate
- Listen to music
- Ride your bike
- Finish a project

Do something that is real, in-the-moment, and positive so that you avoid both the depletion of digital immersion and the secondary feelings of guilt and anxiety that often accompany too much time plugged in.

How cluttered have your devices become?

Digital clutter sneaks up on you because it's not as visible as the clutter in your home. Before you know it, your desktop is littered with icons, your email inbox is overflowing, and your files and documents are so disorganized you need a search party to help you find anything.

If you're like us, your life hinges on the contents of your computer. That may sound dramatic, but if you keep all of your important personal and professional documents and files on your computer, then you know how critical this piece of equipment is to your daily life.

It's so easy to allow our computer lives to become the digital equivalent of *Hoarders*. Trying to locate documents and emails wastes your time and causes daily frustration and anxiety.

Your smartphone is just another mini-computer you drag around with you in your pocket or purse. It's another place for you to horde digital "stuff" that drags you down with excess apps, photos, newsfeeds, and games.

If your devices are bursting at the seams, you feel the weight of that excess whether or not you're aware of it. If you take 10 minutes a day to begin chipping away at the clutter, you'll begin to feel increasingly lighter and unfettered.

We suggest you begin where you'll reap the greatest rewards from de-cluttering your devices. If you are frustrated daily because you can't find a document you need, begin there. If you have heart palpitations every time you see thousands of emails in your inbox, that's the place to start. The key is to just start.

What is your digital mindset?

It's not news to you that your digital devices (or rather the content on them) cause you mental distress and agitation. None of us like to admit it, but we all know how pervasive the digital world has become in our daily lives.

This is not a passing fad that will extinguish over time. It's here to stay, and in all likelihood it will become increasingly prevalent with every passing year. It's up to you to decide how to manage the digital intrusion on your life and the impact on your mental health. It's important to be proactive in your values and choices related to your digital life.

By developing a digital "value system," you create personal boundaries that help you manage your time and clutter (both mental and digital).

Here are some questions to ask yourself that can be used to create digital boundaries:

- How much time each day is absolutely necessary for me to spend on my devices for my job?
- Am I in a job that requires me to spend more time than I want behind my computer?
- How could I interact face-to-face with people in my work more often?
- How much time do I want to spend on my home computer doing work?
- How much time do I want to spend on social media for entertainment?
- How much time do I want to spend on my smartphone for entertainment?
- In what situations is a phone call or personal meeting more appropriate than a text?
- What real-life friendships have I neglected, and how do I want to nurture them?

- What family or relationship agreements should we have in place about using our smartphones, iPads, or laptops in each other's presence?

- What traditions or family time (like dinners together) do you want to make sacred and personal, without the presence of digital devices?

- What limitations or rules should we have for our children's use of digital devices?

- How should I be a role model to my children related to these rules?

- When I have downtime, what are the top five best ways I should use it?

- How can I deal with the urges to "surf the net" or engage in social media when I really don't want to?

- How will I commit to managing my digital clutter so it doesn't get out of hand?

Use your answers to these questions to write down your values and personal commitments related to how you spend your time and energy on and off your devices. You may "fall off the wagon" from time to time, but now you have a wagon to climb back onto!

Simplify Your Activities

"Don't underestimate the value of Doing Nothing, of just going along, listening to all the things you can't hear, and not bothering."

– Winnie the Pooh

How many times have you replied to the question, "How are you?" by answering, "I am so busy. Life is crazy right now?" When was the last time you or someone you know answered the "How are you?" questions with, "Life is great. I'm really relaxed and doing absolutely nothing."

Everyone is in a hurry—doing, doing, doing.

But to what end?

Why are we filling our "to do" lists so we can hurry up and enjoy the leisure time that never seems to materialize?

We feel guilty if our hours aren't packed with "productive" activities that are either income-producing or ego-enlarging. Doing nothing for any extended period feels like failing, even as we continue to develop time-saving technology, gadgets, and devices. The time we gain is quickly sucked up to quell the anxiety created by not enough to do.

According to a 2014 article in *The Economist*, "Individualistic cultures, which emphasize achievement over affiliation, help cultivate this time-is-money mindset. This creates an urgency to make every moment count, notes Harry Triandis, a social psychologist at the University of Illinois."

Do you find yourself running around like a chicken, mindlessly checking items off your list so you feel productive and worthy?

Sometimes our schedules take over our lives, and we don't give much thought to whether or not we are spending our time in ways that contribute to the mental clutter and stress that is so debilitating.

We get trapped on the treadmill of tasks and obligations, leaving little time for those things that allow us to be present and fully engaged.

Omid Safi, Director of Duke University's Islamic Studies Center, in an article for On Being with Krista Tippet, says:

What happened to a world in which we can sit with the people we love so much and have slow conversations about the state of our heart and soul, conversations that slowly unfold, conversations with pregnant pauses and silences that we are in no rush to fill?

How did we create a world in which we have more and more and more to do with less time for leisure, less time for reflection, less time for community, less time to just...be?

There's no doubting the fact that it's hard to break free from the busyness trap. We've been brainwashed to believe that "idleness is the root of all evil." We're not suggesting that working hard, being productive, and having an active life are bad things. To the contrary, they can contribute to a fulfilling, happy life. But there is a diminishing point of return that creates the opposite effect, making you feel depleted and overwhelmed.

Cutting back and expunging non-essential activities can feel uncomfortable, and even threatening at first. If I cut back, what will people think? Will I lose income? Will I appear lazy? Will my kids get behind? Will my world fall apart?

The first step in cutting back is embracing it as a worthy endeavor—acknowledging that busyness is contributing to your mental clutter and accepting that less really can be more.

Here are eight strategies to declutter your schedule so you can enjoy more of what's truly important:

Strategy #1. Prioritize your daily priorities.

Rather than trying to "fit in" your life priorities around your busy schedule, create space for your priorities first. For example, if spending time with your spouse or kids is a priority, then commit to the time you'll spend with them every day. Don't allow that time to be violated without good reasons that you define in advance.

Before you allow a priority to be dislodged for something "really import-ant," take a deep breath and think about it. Does "something important" take precedence over your life priorities?

Strategy #2. Purge your commitments.

Write down all of your personal and professional commitments and tasks for the next week (or month, if you know them). Review the list to see if there are any you can simply drop without serious consequence. Then review the list again to see what you might be able to delegate, delay, or shorten.

If you keep something on the list because you feel guilty, obligated, or uncomfortable, test letting go of it anyway to see what happens. You might discover that you feel liberated, and that the repercussions you feared don't come to pass.

Strategy #3. Focus on three important daily goals.

Rather than trying to accomplish a laundry list of projects and tasks during your day, narrow it down to just three goals. Give yourself per-mission to do less, but with more intention, time, and focus.

You can certainly tackle more if you accomplish your three daily goals, but having just three set in place gives you a sense of control, inner peace, and accomplishment without the feeling of overwhelm and urgency.

Strategy #4. Build in sacred time.

Give yourself time during the day to do absolutely nothing. Sit in a chair and stare out the window, or walk outside and listen to the birds. You don't have to meditate, breathe, plan, ruminate, or "do" anything. Just be.

Try this for five minutes a few times a day. Eventually you may feel comfortable "just being" for an hour or more a day.

Strategy #5. Re-examine your children's schedule.

Parents today aren't as willing as the previous generation of parents to allow their children to have unstructured free time. Kids are over-scheduled with multiple extracurricular activities and pre-planned play dates. Couple this with a much heavier homework load and the enticements of the virtual world, and it's a wonder children spend any time at all in creative play, hanging out with family, or alone with their own imaginations.

Children—especially young children—require plenty of free time for their emotional health and mental development. As with adults, children can suffer from anxiety, depression, and other issues when they feel overwhelmed.

Dorothy Sluss, associate professor of elementary and early childhood education at James Madison University and president of the U.S. chapter of the International Play Association, says that for every week of intensive scheduled activity or sleepaway camp, children need three weeks of less-structured time.

Parents suffer as well from over-scheduling their kids. Spending hours in the car shuffling children from one activity to another is exhausting. Planning various activities for multiple children can have a severe negative impact on your mental energy. The anxiety created by hoping your child excels at t-ball or makes the traveling cheerleading squad only adds to the mental clutter in your life.

It's hard to make the decision to cut back on your child's extracurricular activities, especially in a culture that idolizes competition for even the youngest. But you'll do your child and yourself a favor by finding balance between enrichment activities and complete down time.

Strategy #6. Leave work on time.

According to a recent article in the *Los Angeles Times*, Americans "put in more hours at our jobs than any people in the industrialized world, except Koreans. We take far fewer days of vacation than Europeans. In the last several years, many among us have seen our workload double while our incomes have stayed flat."

But the article goes on the say, "Numerous studies have indicated that people who put in too many hours at their jobs, either by choice or by requirement, become inefficient. With rare exceptions, they burn out and lose their creative edge."

If you are putting in more hours than are required by your job, or you find you're sacrificing other life priorities because of the time you spend working, then you might want to reevaluate your work hours. This is especially important if you're an entrepreneur or work from home as Steve and Barrie do.

Even if you feel passionate about your work, being overwhelmed can still create emotional health problems if you're not balancing it with rest, relationships, and other relaxing activities.

If you work excessive hours, try gradually cutting back, starting with one day a week. Leave work on time, or, if you work from home, turn off your computer at 5:00 pm and commit to leaving it off for the night.

Strategy #7. Take a digital sabbatical.

We've already discussed how excessive digital activities can lead to mental agitation. Even when we're not using our smartphones or laptops, they are always hovering nearby, calling to us to check in on work and see what's happening on Facebook, or luring us to play the latest game app.

Although our parents had plenty of distractions, they didn't have the constant take-your-phone-to-the-bathroom habits we experience today with our devices. It's become more the exception than the norm to see someone walking down the street *without* a cell phone stuck to their ear or in their hands texting.

It may make you hyperventilate to consider this idea, but one of the best ways to gain mental clarity in your life is to frequently take "digital sabbaticals" where you have no access to your cell phone, tablet, computer, or any device that connects you to the Internet.

Start with just one full day or a weekend, or consider using your vacation time as a digital detox where you simply relax and spend time with real people doing real-world activities. If you find that it helps you feel less stressed, then schedule these retreats into your life on a regular basis.

Strategy #8. Harness the power of flow and focus.

Mihaly Csikszentmihalyi (pronounced Me-high Cheek-sent-me-high) is a Hungarian psychologist and pioneer in the work on understanding happiness, creativity, human fulfillment, and the notion of "flow"—a term he coined to describe a state of experience involving heightened focus and immersion in activities such as art, play, and work. He's the author of the bestselling book *Flow: The Psychology of Optimal Experience.*

Cziksentmihalyi defines flow as "a state in which people are so involved in an activity that nothing else seems to matter; the experience is so enjoyable that people will continue to do it even at great cost, for the sheer sake of doing it."

During a "flow" state, a person is completely absorbed in an activity, especially one that involves creative abilities. During this activity, they feel "strong, alert, in effortless control, unselfconscious, and at the peak of their abilities." They are highly focused and undistracted.

Relaxation time spent alone or with family and friends is an excellent antidote to mental clutter, but time spent in the flow state takes it to another level. The flow state can be equated to a meditative state during which you and the activity are one, and your actions feel effortless.

Your mind becomes so absorbed in the activity that you feel transported and almost forget yourself because you are so immersed in the present moment. The flow state, according to Csikszentmihalyi, is the "optimal experience," and the source of our greatest happiness and fulfillment.

He identifies various elements involved in achieving flow, which include:

- There are clear goals every step of the way.
- There is immediate feedback to one's actions.
- There is a balance between challenges and skills.

- Action and awareness are merged.
- Distractions are excluded from consciousness.
- There is no worry of failure.
- Self-consciousness disappears.
- The sense of time becomes distorted.
- The activity becomes an end in itself.

You can achieve flow state by doing the following:

Find a challenge.

Choose an activity that you enjoy doing and find somewhat challenging. It can be anything, whether it's playing the violin, writing your book, doing yoga, playing golf, or focusing on a work project. An activity with a clear set of rules or defined goals makes the challenge better because you can act without questioning what should be done, or how.

Develop your skills.

In order to be able to meet the challenge, you have to develop your skills and become proficient. If the activity is too easy, you'll grow bored quickly, and your mind will wander, preventing you from achieving the flow state. However, if it's too hard, you'll be overwhelmed and you won't be able to achieve that subconscious competence that is necessary for the flow state.

Set clear goals.

You need to be very clear on what you want to achieve with your activity and how you'll know if you're succeeding. For example, you might say, "I'm going to write a chapter in my book. I'll know that I'm succeeding if I define what the chapter will be about, outline the key points I want to make, research the facts I need to include, and know how I'll structure the material."

Focus intently on the task at hand.

In order to maintain a flow state, you'll need to eliminate all other distractions. You don't want anything to pull your attention away from the task or disrupt the state you're in. Once your concentration is broken, you have to rebuild the flow state.

Set aside enough time.

It will take you at least 15 minutes to begin to get into the flow state, and a while longer after that until you feel fully present and immersed in the activity. Once you enter the flow state, you want to have plenty of time to complete your goals and reach the "peak experience."

Monitor your emotional state.

If you're having trouble entering the flow state, monitor your emotions. If you're in an aroused state of anxiety, try a calming exercise like breathing or meditation. If your energy level is low and you're feeling sluggish, do something to invigorate you, such as exercise, eating a healthy snack, or calling a friend. Then go back to your activity and try again.

When you are highly focused in a state of flow, you are fully present with the moment. It's during these moments that your mind is the least cluttered and distracted.

When you find yourself ruminating or agitated, take a few deep calming breaths and begin a flow activity for 30 minutes to an hour or so. Give yourself enough time to become immersed in the activity, and you'll find it has a calming effect on you, in addition to helping you become more productive and happy.

Simplify Your Distractions (to Overcome Procrastination)

"Procrastination is like a credit card: It's a lot of fun until you get the bill."

– Christopher Parker

We all procrastinate, but putting things off until later is one of the worst offenses when it comes to cluttering your mind. When you have something "hanging over your head," you never feel settled or relaxed because it's constantly niggling at you.

In this age of constant distractions, we procrastinate more than ever. The phone buzzes and we look. The email dings and we click over. We have multiple tabs open on our computers luring us away from the task at hand.

Every distraction is a thief, stealing our determination to do what needs to be done or what we deeply desire to achieve. We have all the excuses we need to begin later, to pick it up tomorrow, or to finish as soon as we read just a few more Facebook posts.

Distraction breeds procrastination, but procrastination is also the result of fear—fear of failure or fear of success. It's the great "What if" standing between you and the action you want to take. Even though most of these fears are unfounded, we allow them to pull us away from the task at hand.

We also procrastinate because we dread difficult tasks. We don't want to tax our brains or expend the energy necessary to get started. As you've likely experienced, the getting started part is the most difficult. Once you start, momentum carries you forward, but if you keep procrastinating, you'll never catch that wave of momentum.

Procrastinating not only steals precious time and momentum we could be devoting to achievement, but also our energy and motivation.

The more we procrastinate on something important, the worse we feel about ourselves. The worse we feel, the less motivation we have to get moving on our work. The less motivation we have, the more we procrastinate with mindless distractions. It's a vicious cycle that traps you in self-recriminations and anxiety.

The first step in overcoming procrastination is awareness of the crippling negative impact it has on your mental state.

Think about this: You likely spend at least one hour a day procrastinating. That's seven hours a week—nearly a full workday. So you lose 52 full workdays a year to procrastination. What could you do with an extra 52 workdays?

You could:

- Write a book.
- Start a business.
- Build a blog.
- Go back to school.
- Improve (and build new) personal relationships.
- Teach yourself a new language.
- Finish several big work projects.

If these outcomes have convinced you about the importance of overcoming procrastination, then we recommend the following daily actions to help you get more done during your workweek:

1. Plan ahead.

Before bed or first thing in the morning, determine your first most important task of the day. Then decide on your second and third most important tasks. Make these tasks related to something critical in your work or business—something that will move you forward, make you more money, expand your opportunities. They shouldn't be mindless administrative tasks or filler work.

2. Define your why.

Before you begin your most important task, ask yourself why it's so important. What is the positive motivation for pursuing this task? How will it benefit you? How will you feel when you complete it?

Getting clear on the reasons why you are doing something will help you push through when you begin to feel tired or distracted. You might write down your reasons to have nearby in case you need a reminder.

3. Break it down.

Break down your first most important task into all of the actions and sub-tasks involved in completing the main task. Write down and prioritize every action involved in finishing the task. Then estimate how much time each sub-task will take and write it down.

4. Determine your schedule.

What time of day are you most productive or creative? For Barrie, it's first thing in the morning, when her brain is rested. However, your most productive time might be mid-afternoon. Organize you sub-task priorities to maximize your most productive time.

5. Prepare what you need.

Make sure you have everything you need before you sit down for your work. Get your coffee, water, or tea and have it on your desk. Have a small, healthy snack like almonds, a banana, or some carrots to prevent your stomach from feeling too empty. Make sure the lighting is the way you want it, and your desk is organized or cleared.

6. Repeat the process.

If your priority task of the day only takes a few hours, then move on to task two and repeat the steps above for this. Once you complete task two, do this for task three as well.

7. Remove distractions.

This is hugely important in helping you stay focused. When Barrie was in college, she would go to a "study closet" in her dorm—a tiny closet-sized room with just a desk and a lamp. If she was serious about a project or preparing for a test and didn't want distractions or reasons to procrastinate, that's where she'd go.

Find a space where you can work without interruptions. Turn off your phone. Close all other browsers on your computer, and turn the sound off so you don't hear any dings from emails. Put a "do not disturb" sign on your office door.

8. Begin with mindfulness.

Before you begin your first sub-task of your most important task for the day, close your eyes, take a few deep breaths, and set an intention that you will complete your task easily and productively. Visualize yourself accomplishing it and how you will feel when you're done. But try not to use this moment as another reason to procrastinate. Instead, make it a one – to two-minute mental preparation to begin your work.

9. Set a timer.

If you have a hard time focusing, set a timer for 20–30 minutes (or less if you have a really hard time focusing). Work diligently during that time, and when the timer goes off, allow yourself a short break to stretch, walk outside, close your eyes, or whatever feels rejuvenating. Try not to use this time to check emails, get on a long phone call, or do anything that will steal your productive time.

One strategy that Steve uses to create extreme focus (using a timer) is The Pomodoro Technique, where you focus on a single task for 25 minutes, take a 5-minute break, and then begin another 25-minute block of time. This strategy can be grueling at times, but it also helps him stay laser-focused on his most important activities.

10. Schedule longer breaks.

In between your three most important tasks, schedule longer breaks of 15 minutes to an hour (for lunch). Use these breaks to re-energize by doing some exercise or meditation, or by having a non-stressful conversation with someone.

11. Reward yourself.

After you complete a task or a series of sub-tasks, reward yourself with either the breaks mentioned earlier or allowing yourself to check your phone, emails, or social media for a short amount of time (10 to 15 minutes). Or do something else that feels rewarding and motivating.

12. Schedule mindless tasks.

Beyond your three most important tasks of the day, you will certainly have mindless tasks to accomplish. If you must check emails first thing in the morning, allow yourself a short amount of time to do so (10 to 15 minutes).

Set a timer, and even if you haven't completed going through the emails, stop for now, move on to your most important task, and come back to the emails later in the day when you've completed your tasks. Other mindless tasks like easy paperwork, organizing, or anything that doesn't take much brainpower can be scheduled at your least productive times of day.

Simplify Your Actions

"Drink your tea slowly and reverently, as if it's the axis on which the earth revolves–slowly, evenly, without rushing toward the future; live the actual moment. Only this moment is life."

– Thích Nhat Hanh

What if you could always be in the state of flow described earlier, where time disappears and you are one with the activity? Perhaps this would be a blissful, transformative state to live in—but you might starve, forget to pay your bills, and neglect to shower.

Real life requires that you deal with the more mundane but necessary activities of daily survival in an organized society. They are the tasks we try to "get through" in order to enjoy the real excitement of life, whatever that happens to be for you.

Unless you're a cave dweller or live in a monastery, these "real-life" obligations take up a lot of time and energy. Even if you can cut back on these tasks, you can't escape all of them without some unpleasant consequences.

But maybe escaping them really isn't necessary in order to declutter your mind and enjoy more of life. What if you brought mindfulness to everything you do, including the unpleasant, boring, or neutral activities of ordinary life?

As Thích Nhat Hanh suggests in the quote above, rather than slurping down your tea while thinking about all you have to do today, shift your perspective to see drinking your tea as the *only* important thing in the world (while you are drinking it). This shift would apply to everything you do—from washing the dishes to cleaning out the cat box.

Maybe you don't want to be present when cleaning the cat box, but presence is the state of mind you want to seek in *everything* you do.

Is it possible to be present all of the time? Not really. But you can try. And if you succeed in living mindfully just a little more often, you'll discover that the joy and peace you seek is at your fingertips all the time.

Let's examine five ways you can bring mindfulness into your daily life to become present and aware even during the most mundane activities.

#1. Eat meals mindfully.

Once upon a time, people used to spend hours producing and preparing food. They would stop in the middle of a day for a big meal called "dinner," when everyone would leave work and sit down together to eat. Later on, dinner happened in the evening, but still it was an occasion when people sat together and spent time eating and talking.

With the advent of fast food, technology, and multi-tasking, eating is often relegated to a quick meal between obligations, something necessary to keep us fueled for our over-scheduled lives. Not only do we neglect the ritual of family meals, but too often we overlook the simple joy of eating.

We may not have as much time to focus on food preparation as our grandmothers did, but we can be mindful of the food we eat and how we experience a meal. This means not eating in front of the TV or computer, but rather sitting with your family or alone in a quiet, distraction-free place.

Here are a few thoughts on mindful eating:

- Before you eat, look at the food and notice the colors, smells, and textures.
- Close your eyes and breathe in the aromas.
- Notice your own hunger and urge to eat.
- When you put the first bite of food into your mouth, notice the immediate tastes and sensations.
- As you chew, notice how the tastes might change or expand.
- Chew and swallow your food slowly, with a thought of gratitude for the hands that prepared it.

- As you continue to eat, notice how your stomach feels as you satiate your appetite.
- Be aware of feeling full, and cease eating when you are. Don't feel obliged to overeat in order to clean your plate.
- After you finish the meal, sit for a few moments and digest your food.
- After the meal, mindfully wash your plate and utensils and put them away.

When you eat mindfully, not only will you savor the experience of eating, but you'll also support proper digestion and absorption of nutrients. Studies show eating slowly leads to improved satiety and reduced calorie intake.

#2. Clean your house mindfully.

Thích Nhat Hanh has said that he washes dishes with as much care as if he were bathing the newborn Buddha: "If I am incapable of washing dishes joyfully, if I want to finish them quickly so I can go and have a cup of tea, then I will be incapable of drinking the tea joyfully."

Rather than organizing your house as a means to a decluttered mind, focus on the doing rather than the getting it done. Cleaning won't magically become an elevated experience, but you will be elevated by simply paying attention to the elegant cause and effect of cleaning. Try to see housecleaning as a laboratory for being present and engaged in life.

This mind shift can be applied to any routine task—washing your car, mowing the lawn, or even paying the bills. You can approach these tasks with dread and resentment, or you can approach them with your full attention and a sense of gratitude that you are able to accomplish them, that they improve your life, and that, however insignificant, they are worthy of your time.

#3. Walk mindfully.

As Barrie writes in her book *Peace of Mindfulness*, "Taking a walk, you can be mindful by listening intently to your feet hitting the ground, and the sounds of nature around you. Take in the scenery you observe, the feeling of the warm or cool air, and the smells of being outside."

Wherever you are walking (either indoors or out), whatever your destination, pay attention along the way. You don't have to hustle along with your eye on the outcome. Let walking be the destination.

#4. Experience nature mindfully.

Numerous studies have shown the mental and physical benefits of spending time in nature. Being in forests and green spaces can:

- Boost the immune system
- Lower blood pressure
- Reduce stress
- Improve your mood
- Increase your ability to focus
- Accelerate recovery from surgery or illness
- Increase your energy level
- Improve your sleep

You will experience these benefits simply by taking a walk in nature or sitting quietly in a forest. But when you approach your experience of nature mindfully, you'll enhance the benefits—particularly related to stress reduction, mood, and focus.

When you spend time in nature, try to pay attention with all of your senses to be fully present and attentive to your surroundings.

Listen…to the sounds of the birds, the leaves rustling in the trees, the water running over stones.

See…the sunlight and shadows, the tiny wildflowers on the forest floor, the hawk flying in circles overhead.

Smell…the earthy scent of rotting leaves, the fragrance of honeysuckle, the aroma of a recent rain shower.

The experience of being in green spaces and forests is so powerful and mind-clearing that it should be part of your Declutter Your Mind practice.

#5. Exercise mindfully.

The benefits of exercise are so numerous we could fill an entire book with them. The physical benefits are obvious, but related to your mental declutter efforts, exercise has some profound psychological benefits as well.

Michael Otto, PhD, a professor of psychology at Boston University in an article for the American Psychological Association, says "The link between exercise and mood is pretty strong. Usually within five minutes after moderate exercise you get a mood-enhancement effect."

The article goes on to say that studies confirm exercise can treat and perhaps prevent anxiety and depression, both of which are potential outcomes of mental clutter, distraction, and rumination.

Even with the overwhelming evidence that exercise makes you healthier, fitter, and happier, most people avoid it like the plague. Exercise can feel like a chore at best, and like physical torture to some people. Part of the problem is the way we approach exercise. We see it as a means to an end—to lose weight, to manage stress, or to prevent disease.

We've learned that once you remove judgment, attachments, and fear from the equation, fitness can be something to look forward to rather than an obligation you dread. You no longer anticipate the discomfort, think constantly about quitting, or judge your results. You simply engage in mindful movement, pushing yourself slightly to improve each time, while paying full attention to your body.

No matter what activity or sport you practice, you can incorporate mindfulness into your practice to maximize a clear, focused mind.

Try these ideas:

Pay attention to your body.

As you start your exercise practice, pay attention to the placement of your body. Is your posture correct? Is everything aligned as it should be around your core?

Your core is the center of strength and support, and for it to operate efficiently, your body must be aligned, with your back straight, shoulders back, and head held high (unless the exercise calls for something else).

Allow your core do most of the work, while your limbs are fluid and relaxed. Even if you're lifting weights with your arms or legs, engage your core to add power to your limbs. As you exercise, focus on engaging your core, and envision an imaginary steel rod keeping your body in proper alignment.

Focus on how your body feels. Are you experiencing any pain or discomfort? Without reacting to the feelings, simply identify them. "My knees are hurting. I'm having trouble catching my breath. It's hot out here." Try not to resist or fear any pain or discomfort, but rather breathe into it and visualize it relaxing.

Picture sending energy or power to whatever part of your body is performing the work of the exercise. If several parts are moving at once, spread the energy throughout your body.

Find your anchor.

Once you are in the groove of the movements of your exercise, find an anchor to hold your focus. Place your attention on your breathing, the sounds of nature, or a mantra you repeat to yourself. For example, while running, you could focus on the sound of your feet hitting the pavement. You could also mentally repeat a mantra or affirmation that matches your breathing pattern.

During strength training exercises, vividly focus on the muscles you're training and the energy surrounding those areas. Follow your breathing, breathe out as you lift or engage the weight, and breathe in when you lower it. Stay focused on your breathing, even in between lifts.

When thoughts intrude, just return your attention back to your mantra or breathing, or take a moment to access how your body feels and adjust or relax as necessary. Then go back to breathing or your mantra.

Notice your environment.

No matter where you are exercising (indoors or out), pay attention to the temperature, sights, sounds, smells, and any other sensory perceptions that impact your experience. Pull your focus from inside of you to your surroundings and notice everything around you.

If you are outside, allow yourself to enjoy the dual psychological benefits of being in nature and exercising as you give your full attention to your surroundings.

Every moment of every day, you can easily be sucked back into the vortex of your thoughts and distractions. You can be staring at a glorious star-filled sky or putting dishes in the dishwasher and be completely unconscious of the experience because of your cluttered mind.

Sholto Radford, founder of Wilderness Minds retreats, says "The practice of mindfulness invites us to let go of goals and expectations and see what emerges in the space left when the striving mind quiets for a moment."

Your job is to awaken, even if it's for just a few moments every day, to truly experience your experiences—to be fully present and aware rather than tangled up in your thoughts and worries. With practice and time, you'll find returning to the present moment becomes more automatic. And the more you return to it, the more life you are actually living.

CONCLUSION

Final Thoughts on Decluttering Your Mind

"Your mind is the basis of everything you experience and of every contribution you make to the lives of others. Given this fact, it makes sense to train it."

– Sam Harris

Training your mind is the mental equivalent of tidying your house. It's a habit you must repeat daily in order to stay on top of it. But training your mind is not as straightforward or simple as housekeeping.

Managing your thoughts takes commitment and practice. It also requires daily—even moment-by-moment—awareness of your mental state and the shenanigans of your monkey mind.

Left to its own devices, your mind will swing from branch to branch, following an old memory, chasing a distraction, or stewing in the bitter juice of resentment or anger. Or it can languish in daydreaming and fantasy, much more positive but still unruly states of mind. When you neglect to take stock of your mental clutter, your thoughts and emotions remain freewheeling and capricious. As a result, your experience of life becomes unpredictable and entirely dependent on the random nature of thought.

The intrusive thoughts you experience throughout the day illustrate the maddening reality that many of the functions of the mind seem outside of conscious control. To add insult to injury, our thoughts *feel* very real and powerful and have a profound impact on our perceptions of the world.

For a moment, let go of the notion that your spontaneous thoughts have any meaning. What if those intrusive thoughts have no more truth or substance than random graffiti on a wall? There may be some connection to a memory or emotion, but in the present moment they don't reflect reality. For the most part, this is the truth about thoughts.

Although your subconscious mind will never allow you to have complete control of your thoughts, you do have the ability to control some of them. And you can change your reactions and habits in order to better manage them and the emotions they foster.

Throughout this book, we have offered a wide-range selection of ideas and tools for decluttering your mind so you can quiet the negative voice in your head, experience less stress, and enjoy more peace of mind.

With focused breathing and mindfulness meditation, you trigger the relaxation response and learn to detach from intrusive thoughts and emotions.

By interrupting, reframing, and challenging thoughts, you learn to take charge of your thinking and diminish the power thoughts have over you.

When you identify your core values, you create boundaries for your choices and actions so you don't give yourself more reason to ruminate and worry.

Once you clarify your life priorities, you don't waste your time on things that will later cause you regret or mental suffering.

When you set goals based on your values and priorities, you set the stage for focused action and self-esteem that keeps you feeling energized.

When you seek out and live your passion, you infuse your goals with authenticity, purpose, and joy, leaving little room for negative thinking.

By being more present and mindful in your relationships, you prevent many of the conflicts that come with human interaction, minimizing the resulting mental distress and increasing fulfillment with the relationship.

When you keep your home and your digital world clean, organized, and streamlined, you remove distractions that pull you away from your values, priorities, and goals.

By making the decision to cut back on tasks and obligations, you reduce stress, allowing more "space" to be present and attentive to life.

As you focus on the task at hand and involve yourself in "flow" activities, you transcend the mental chatter in your head to become one with the activity, fostering feelings of joy and deep satisfaction.

When you tackle procrastination and learn to quickly take the first step, you circumvent the anxiety that comes with putting things off.

By applying mindfulness to all of the daily activities of life, from dishwashing to exercise, you clear your mind of all but the only true reality in life—the present moment. American psychologist Abraham Maslow says, "The ability to be in the present moment is a major component of mental wellness."

So how do you decide where to begin your mental declutter practice?

We suggest you begin by first defining your core values, life priorities, and goals. Once you have these personal boundaries and directives established, you'll find it much easier to determine where you have the most disruptive mental clutter and how you want to deal with it.

For example, if you have a core value of building strong relationships, but you find yourself in regular conflict with someone or constantly brooding over a relationship encounter, then the relationship exercises we outlined are a great place to begin your mental declutter.

Or you may find yourself constantly disparaging your abilities or appearance, and these negative thoughts prevent you from enjoying life. If this is the case, working on self-acceptance, ending comparisons, and forgiveness might be the place to begin.

Some of the practices we outlined, like breathing, meditation, simplifying, and daily mindfulness, can be applied or practiced for short periods of time every day. The results from these practices will help you with the more complex endeavors, such as improving relationships, overcoming the past, or finding your passion.

We also suggest you keep a journal to document the mental declutter practices you undertake, and how your life and emotions improve as a result. By tracking your actions and the resulting changes that occur, you'll feel inspired and motivated to continue with your mental decluttering efforts.

Decluttering your mind is a lifelong endeavor, but one that pays off with profound rewards that can significantly impact your quality of life. The less time you spend "in your head" with intrusive, negative thoughts, the more time you have to enjoy the present moment—and every present moment for the rest of your life.

You understand what it takes to feel less anxious about all the "stuff" that goes on inside your head. Now, we urge you to take action. Start today with the biggest challenge in your life and commit to fixing in the next week. If you get stuck, use the eight-step process that Steve recommends for building a new habit (http://bit.ly/2aBWv0K). Simply, identify the exercise that will help overcome this challenge and then create a routine for doing it on a daily basis.

We wish you the best of luck!

Barrie Davenport

Steve Scott

400 Words That Identify Your Values (Bonus Section)

Your core values are the guiding principles of your life that help you determine your behavior, words, and actions. It's essential to your personal evolution to take stock of your values on a regular basis, and then make the necessary changes to align your life with these most critical values.

Living in harmony with your values creates a fertile environment for happiness, peace of mind, and success, because you are living authentically without confusion, guilt, or shame. Even small, incremental changes to align your life with your values will create a positive shift in your feelings and attitude.

Look at this list of 400 value words below, and select your top 5 to 10 for your personal and professional life.

Write them down and evaluate how you might be living outside of your values right now. What do you need to change to support your values? What is the first step you can take today?

Ability	Abundance
Acceptance	Accomplishment
Achievement	Acknowledgement
Adaptability	Adequacy
Adroitness	Adventure
Affection	Affluence
Alertness	Aliveness
Ambition	Amusement
Anticipation	Appreciation

Approachability

Artfulness

Articulacy

Assertiveness

Assurance

Attentiveness

Attractiveness

Audacity

Availability

Awareness

Awe

Balance

Beauty

Being-ness

Belongingness

Benevolence

Blissfulness

Boldness

Bravery

Brilliance

Briskness

Buoyancy

Calmness

Camaraderie

Candor

Capability

Care

Carefulness

Certainty

Challenge

Charity

Charm

Chastity

Cheerfulness

Clarity

Classy

Cleanliness

Cleverness

Closeness

Cognizance

Comfort

Commitment

Compassion

Competence

Completion

Composure

Concentration

Confidence

Conformity

Congruency

Connection

Consistency

Continuity

Control

Conviviality

Cooperation

Cordiality

Courage

Craftiness

Credibility

Curiosity

Decisiveness

Deepness

Delicacy

Dependability

Desire

Devotion

Dexterity

Diligence

Direction

Discernment

Discipline

Diversity

Drive

Dynamism

Consciousness

Contentment

Contribution

Conviction

Coolness

Copiousness

Correctness

Courtesy

Creativity

Cunning

Daring

Decorum

Deference

Delight

Depth

Determination

Devoutness

Dignity

Diplomacy

Directness

Discretion

Discovery

Dreaming

Duty

Eagerness

Economy

Education

Efficiency

Elegance

Encouragement

Energy

Enlightenment

Enthusiasm

Exactness

Excitement

Expectancy

Experience

Exploration

Extravagance

Exuberance

Fairness

Fame

Fashion

Fidelity

Finesse

Fitness

Flow

Fluidity

Fortitude

Freedom

Ecstasy

Effectiveness

Elation

Empathy

Endurance

Enjoyment

Entertainment

Evolution

Excellence

Exhilaration

Expediency

Expertise

Expressiveness

Extroversion

Facilitating

Faith

Fascination

Fearlessness

Fineness

Firmness

Flexibility

Fluency

Focus

Frankness

Friendliness

Frugality

Gallantry

Gentility

Giving

Gratefulness

Gregariousness

Guidance

Harmony

Heart

Heroism

Honesty

Hopefulness

Humility

Hygiene

Impact

Impeccability

Industry

Inquisitiveness

Inspiration

Integrity

Intensity

Intrepidness

Intuition

Inventiveness

Judiciousness

Fun

Generosity

Genuineness

Grace

Gratitude

Growth

Happiness

Health

Helpfulness

Holiness

Honor

Hospitality

Humor

Imagination

Impartiality

Independence

Ingenuity

Insightfulness

Instinctiveness

Intelligence

Intimacy

Introversion

Intuitiveness

Joy

Justice

Keenness	Kindness
Knowledge	Lavishness
Leadership	Learning
Liberation	Liberty
Liveliness	Logic
Longevity	Love
Loyalty	Majesty
Mastery	Maturity
Meekness	Mellowness
Meticulousness	Mindfulness
Moderation	Modesty
Motivation	Mysteriousness
Neatness	Nerve
Obedience	Open-mindedness
Openness	Optimism
Opulence	Order
Organization	Originality
Outlandishness	Outrageousness
Passion	Peacefulness
Perceptiveness	Perfection
Perseverance	Persistence
Persuasiveness	Philanthropy
Piety	Playfulness
Pleasantness	Pleasure
Plentiful-ness	Poise

Polish	Popularity
Potency	Practicality
Pragmatism	Precision
Preeminence	Preparedness
Presence	Privacy
Proactivity	Proficiency
Professionalism	Prosperity
Prudence	Punctuality
Purity	Qualification
Quietness	Quickness
Realism	Readiness
Reason	Recognition
Recreation	Refinement
Reflection	Relaxation
Reliability	Resilience
Resolution	Resolve
Resourcefulness	Respect
Restfulness	Restraint
Reverence	Richness
Rigor	Sacredness
Sacrifice	Sagacity
Saintliness	Sanguinity
Satisfaction	Security
Self-control	Selflessness
Self-realization	Self-reliance

Sensitivity

Sensuality

Serenity

Service

Sexuality

Sharing

Shrewdness

Significance

Silence

Silliness

Simplicity

Sincerity

Skillfulness

Smartness

Sophistication

Solidarity

Solidity

Solitude

Soundness

Speed

Spirit

Spirituality

Spontaneity

Stability

Stillness

Strength

Structure

Substantiality

Success

Sufficiency

Support

Supremacy

Surprise

Superbness

Sympathy

Synergy

Tactfulness

Teamwork

Temperance

Thankfulness

Thoroughness

Thoughtfulness

Thrift

Tidiness

Timeliness

Traditionalism

Tranquility

Transcendence

Trust

Trustworthiness

Truth	Understanding
Uniqueness	Unity
Usefulness	Utility
Valor	Variety
Victory	Vigor
Virtue	Vision
Vitality	Vivacity
Warmth	Watchfulness
Wealth	Wholesomeness
Willfulness	Willingness
Winning	Wisdom
Wittiness	Wonder
Worthiness	Zeal
Zest	Zing

Did You Like *Declutter Your Mind?*

Before you go, we'd like to say "thank you" for purchasing our book.

You could have picked from dozens of books on habit development, but you took a chance and checked out this one.

So a big thanks for downloading this book and reading all the way to the end.

Now we'd like ask for a *small* favor. **Could you please take a minute or two and leave a review for this book on Amazon?**

This feedback will help us continue to write the kind of Kindle books that help you get results. And if you loved it, then please let us know :-)

MORE BOOKS BY BARRIE

- 10-Minute Digital Declutter: The Simple Habit to Eliminate Technology Overload
- 10-Minute Declutter: The Stress-Free Habit for Simplifying Your Home
- 201 Relationship Questions: The Couple's Guide to Building Trust and Emotional Intimacy
- Self-Discovery Questions: 155 Breakthrough Questions to Accelerate Massive Action
- Sticky Habits: 6 Simple Steps To Create Good Habits That Stick
- Peace of Mindfulness: Everyday Rituals to Conquer Anxiety and Claim Unlimited Inner Peace
- Confidence Hacks: 99 Small Actions to Massively Boost Your Confidence
- Building Confidence: Get Motivated, Overcome Social Fear, Be Assertive, and Empower Your Life For Success
- The 52-Week Life Passion Project: Uncover Your Life Passion

All of Barrie's books can be found at:
liveboldandbloom.com/barrie-davenport-books

MORE BOOKS BY STEVE

- The Miracle Morning for Writers: How to Build a Writing Ritual That Increases Your Impact and Your Income
- 10-Minute Digital Declutter: The Simple Habit to Eliminate Technology Overload
- 10-Minute Declutter: The Stress-Free Habit for Simplifying Your Home
- Crowdsource Your Success: How Accountability Helps You Stick to Goals
- Confident You: An Introvert's Guide to Success in Life and Business
- Exercise Enough: 32 Tactics for Building the Exercise Habit (Even If You Hate Working Out)
- The Daily Entrepreneur: 33 Success Habits for Small Business Owners, Freelancers and Aspiring 9-to-5 Escape Artists
- Master Evernote: The Unofficial Guide to Organizing Your Life with Evernote (Plus 75 Ideas for Getting Started)
- Bad Habits No More: 25 Steps to Break ANY Bad Habit
- Habit Stacking: 97 Small Life Changes That Take Five Minutes or Less
- To-Do List Makeover: A Simple Guide to Getting the Important Things Done
- 23 Anti-Procrastination Habits: How to Stop Being Lazy and Get Results in Your Life
- S.M.A.R.T. Goals Made Simple: 10 Steps to Master Your Personal and Career Goals
- 115 Productivity Apps to Maximize Your Time: Apps for iPhone, iPad, Android, Kindle Fire and PC/iOS Desktop Computers

- Writing Habit Mastery: How to Write 2,000 Words a Day and Forever Cure Writer's Block
- Declutter Your Inbox: 9 Proven Steps to Eliminate Email Overload
- Wake Up Successful: How to Increase Your Energy and Achieve Any Goal with a Morning Routine
- 10,000 Steps Blueprint: The Daily Walking Habit for Healthy Weight Loss and Lifelong Fitness
- 70 Healthy Habits: How to Eat Better, Feel Great, Get More Energy and Live a Healthy Lifestyle
- Resolutions That Stick! How 12 Habits Can Transform Your New Year

All of Steve's books can be found at: <u>www.developgoodhabits.com</u>

ABOUT STEVE

In his books, S.J. Scott provides daily action plans for every area of your life: health, fitness, work and personal relationships. Unlike other personal development guides, his content focuses on taking action. So instead of reading over-hyped strategies that rarely work in the real-world, you'll get information that can be immediately implemented.

ABOUT BARRIE

Barrie is the founder of an award-winning personal development site, Live Bold and Bloom (liveboldandbloom.com). She is a certified personal coach and online course creator, helping people apply practical, evidence-based solutions and strategies to push past comfort zones and create happier, richer, more successful lives. She is also the author of a series of self-improvement books on positive habits, life passion, confidence building, mindfulness and simplicity.

As an entrepreneur, a mom of three and a homeowner, Barrie know firsthand how valuable and life-changing it is to simplify, prioritize an organize your daily habits in order to live your best life.

9 781535 575089